The Power of Focus:
Lessons Learned in District and School Improvement

The Power of Focus: Lessons Learned in District and School Improvement

Jeff Nelsen, Joe Palumbo,
Amalia Cudeiro, and Jan Leight

To order additional copies of this book, contact:
Focus on Results
1-888-743-1076
www.focusonresults.net
28921

CONTENTS

Dedication

We dedicate this book to our parents and family members
who have supported us for so many years in this challenging work.

Foreword

Focus on Results is a powerful tool for improvement in schools and districts. As Superintendent of Edmonton Public Schools in Edmonton, Alberta, Canada, I have seen the Focus framework and strategies improve the work of our staff and more importantly, the measured student achievement results of our students. The concepts and strategies of the Focus framework detailed in this book are solid, practical, action oriented and actually *useable*. They help schools and districts figure out how to get the work done to improve student achievement and high school completion.

In Edmonton, we launched our partnership in the fall of 2000 when we found out that our test scores had generally stagnated and our high school completion rates were close to the bottom of the rest of the province. Together, with the Focus on Results Team, we developed a pilot in twenty six schools that included ongoing training and on-site coaching to support school leadership teams in implementing the Seven Areas of Focus. The pilot schools made such progress in the first year that we expanded the work of Focus on Results to include all 208 schools in the district.

Our district office also committed to the important work of focus, and realigned all of our efforts to support one specific goal: superb results from all students and high school completion. The Focus on Results team provided monthly executive on and off site coaching to me and my senior leadership to

- design an Edmonton-based targeted professional development plan for all principals and teachers that centers around the instructional focus and researched-based teaching strategies,

- re-orient district office support around issues of teaching and learning, and
- develop principal and district office staff capacity as instructional leaders.

The Focus on Results team proved essential in helping our district services and school leadership teams learn how to do our jobs more effectively. They are also helping us to make brave decisions that are in the best interests of our students and student learning results.

Three years later, student achievement is improving with real, measurable results. We are showing demonstrated growth on both provincially mandated achievement tests and high school completion rates.

These successes are the result of both the dedicated efforts from our staff, and the support of the framework and strategies outlined in this book. I am confident that the Focus on Results team and the framework, combined with a sincere desire to improve will lead to the same results. Our results are public and our books are open.

Angus McBeath
Superintendent
Edmonton Public Schools,
Alberta, Canada

Acknowledgments

We want to begin by thanking the staffs and communities where we were teachers, principals, and central office staff and learned so much about our work as educators: Long Beach Unified School District (USD), Baldwin Park USD, and Ventura, USD.

We are also extremely grateful to the dedicated families, teachers, principals, and central office staffs of our partner districts who work tirelessly to implement the ideas of this book so they may positively impact the learning and lives of their students and who have allowed us to work and learn alongside them.

Also, thank you to the entire Focus on Results staff for your insight and hard work as you support educators in implementing the framework in districts and schools throughout North America.

Finally, we are extremely grateful to our funders who have supported us in developing, researching, and implementing our framework, including the Ball Foundation, Stupski Family Foundation, Broad Foundation, Department of Defense, Education Development Center, Disney Learning Partnership, and Boston Plan for Excellence.

Introduction

We have all been there. As principals of typical "underperforming schools," the four of us were daunted by the challenges shared across our different schools and districts. Our students had a limited proficiency in English, low standardized test scores, lived in poverty, and were unsupported at home. Many of our teachers were demoralized from years of exhausting hours, changing reform efforts from the turnstile of superintendents, and lack of real support. It was hard enough getting the building's heat turned on, much less tackling student performance. Yet somehow, we were each able to support our students in moving from an average of 15th percentile to 90th percentile in reading, math, and language arts.

After several years of such successes, we were each asked independently to come to the University of California at Los Angeles (UCLA) to take on the challenge of working with Project LEARN and the three hundred lowest-performing schools in LA Unified. As we met and then worked together at UCLA, we wrestled with how best to help the committed leadership at these struggling schools and shared the stories of our own past successes.

It was amazing to us how similar our stories were. We came to believe that there were certain actions, steps, and strategies that, taken together and implemented well, could make a powerful impact on student learning. We began to organize our thinking and experience and to create tools to help schools with implementing key areas. Eventually, the four of us formed Focus on Results and started on the journey that has led us to this point.

Focus on Results is a consulting group comprised of successful practitioners, all of whom have been in leadership positions in schools and districts that have shown dramatic improvement in student learning. The four authors of this book have a combined one hundred plus years of experience leading and learning from students, teachers, principals, and central office staff as we worked together to improve the school performance.

The purpose of this book is to share the lessons we have learned from our research, study, and experience in hopes that it will not only help individual schools and districts improve but will further the dialogue on what it takes to build more successful school experiences for all children. We share these lessons by detailing the *framework* and *strategies* we have developed that are based on our successful experience in the field.

Framework. Focus on Results has developed a framework for school improvement called the "Seven Areas of Focus." We first began to define and clarify the meaning of the areas during our work with the Boston Plan for Excellence and Boston Public Schools (BPS) in Massachusetts between 1996 and 1999. As BPS schools implemented the framework, we were able to further refine and develop the areas based on school and district feedback as well as our own study of the framework's impact on school improvement efforts.

During the subsequent years, BPS adopted a version of this model, and the implementation of this framework is given partial credit for some of the systemwide gains that district is experiencing under Superintendent Tom Payzant. The version we present today has continued to evolve as new information and experience shape it.

The Seven Areas of Focus are as follows:

Area 1:   Identify and implement a schoolwide Instructional Focus.
Area 2:   Develop professional collaboration teams to improve teaching and learning.

Area 3:   Identify, learn, and use effective evidence-based teaching practices.

Area 4:   Create a targeted professional development plan that builds expertise in selected evidence-based practices.

Area 5:   Realign resources (people, time, talent, energy, and money) to support the Instructional Focus.

Area 6:   Engage families and the community in supporting the Instructional Focus.

Area 7:   Create an internal accountability system growing out of student learning goals that promote measurable gains in learning for every student.

We acknowledge that this is not the only framework available—it may not even be the best framework for every situation. However, the Seven Areas of Focus is unique in that it is the only framework that is *comprehensive, data driven, and instructionally focused.*

First, our framework is *comprehensive* in that it incorporates all of the elements that research and experience suggest are critical to school improvement. While there are individual books and papers that provide thoughts on particular aspects of this framework, this book details *all* of these components in a way that is clear, integrated, and action-oriented.

Second, our framework is *data driven.* The key to implementing this framework is to use data to inform important decisions. Multiple sources of data are used ranging from standardized test scores, local student measures, and samples of student work to research on effective teaching strategies, budget information, and even feedback from the community.

Finally, our framework is distinctive because it revolves around one *single* "Instructional Focus." We ask staffs to choose one specific instructional area of the academic curriculum they believe is the most important for students to know to be successful in life. It is essential to note, an Instructional Focus is NOT simply a "focus on instruction." Instead, it is what the school staff does excellently, expertly, and in every classroom for every student.

While other improvement efforts and comprehensive school reform models include several components of the Seven Areas of Focus, our research has found that the most successful efforts are organized around one single Instructional Focus. We will examine this component in great detail in chapter 1. A summary of some of the relevant research that supports each area of the framework is located at the end of this book.

Strategies. While this book shares field-tested strategies throughout, two overarching components of our work—*implementation embedded in local context and culture and shifting from a traditional central office to a central services organization*—weave across all areas of the framework.

First, implementation of the framework is *embedded in local context and culture.* Instead of opening a handbook to learn how to implement an off-the-shelf reform model, the school and district staffs develop the details of improvement plans themselves, often with the support of a facilitator. This empowers individuals and builds momentum for the work. Staffs develop their strategies using the framework, but the details are based on their own strengths, abilities, and needs. Staffs are more empowered because they are the source of the real change and improvement.

Second, the framework itself is only effective when accompanied by a *shift from a traditional central office to a central services organization.* We have multiple examples of how the framework has led to dramatic improvement in student learning in districts that become customer-service-driven central services organizations and fully support school-level implementation. We have also seen a few other examples of districts where the traditional central office did not provide leadership, causing schools to halfheartedly embrace the framework and continue at their previous performance levels.

Both overarching and specific strategies for implementing the framework are detailed to give the reader specific ideas of how to turn the lessons we learned into concrete change in their school or district. Numerous districts and schools in a variety of states and countries around the world have found these strategies to be helpful in improving learning in students from a wide variety of backgrounds, races, and economic situations.

How to Use This Book

We want school and central office staff to *use* this book. This is not meant to simply sit on the shelf as another interesting perspective on how schools might change. Instead, it is meant to jump-start conversations about how to improve and it actually provides tools, examples, and strategies for taking action toward improvement. Perhaps your school is implementing much of the framework already but needs an Instructional Focus by which to organize your work. Perhaps your district is ready to approach change on a sweeping scale and needs support in all areas. Regardless of your specific needs, we hope you will reflect upon these thoughts and take whatever is helpful and apply it to your individual work.

The following chapters discuss our framework and associated strategies that support improved student learning. First, we discuss the Seven Areas of Focus in great detail including the following:

- **Foundations**—Understand the fundamental components of each area of focus and what they look like in a school or district.
- **Getting Started**—Examine the most effective strategies for launching this work in schools and districts, including lessons learned, challenges, and examples of real schools and districts working using the framework.
- **District Support**—Successful school improvement cannot be undertaken without the full support of the district. Learn specific strategies and examples of ways districts can support the very challenging work of their schools.

- **Tools for Leaders**—Find concrete exercises, documents, and activities to help you implement these strategies in your schools and districts.

The details of the framework are followed by discussion on the possibilities for improvement and how you *can* achieve your goals through leadership and district improvement.

While this book is based in the research and literature about school and district improvement, it is designed for the practitioner-at-heart, whose passion is to see dramatic improvement in student learning as quickly as possible. By applying the framework, strategies, and beliefs of Focus on Results, we intend for others to experience the same gains that we have seen.

Chapter 1

Area 1: Identify and Implement a Schoolwide Instructional Focus

FOUNDATIONS

Area 1: Identify and implement a schoolwide Instructional Focus.

- An Instructional Focus is the one specific academic area of the curriculum the staff has chosen as most important for its students to know and do to be successful in their academic work.

- An Instructional Focus is based on every student's learning needs as evidenced by multiple sources of data that has been disaggregated by various student groups.

- An Instructional Focus touches the whole school—every professional, every classroom, every day.

- The principal and staff hold each other mutually accountable and expect every student to show growth in the area of the Instructional Focus. Any excuses for low performance based on race, gender, ethnicity, primary language, socio-economic level, or class factors are unacceptable.

- **An Instructional Focus is the one specific academic area of the curriculum the staff has chosen as most important for its students to know and do to be successful in their academic work.**

While there is no specific order to approach the Seven Areas of Focus, this area does come first, and it drives all other work. The importance of focusing on one instructional area cannot be overly stressed. Plato is often attributed as being the first to say, "The Good is the eternal enemy of the Best." In our experience, schools are faced with so many issues, so many good programs, and so many important activities that they tend to be ruled by the *tyranny of the urgent*—i.e., they react first to put out immediate fires and then spend time on more critical long-term goals.

In our experience, we have discovered that one key to high performing or rapidly improving schools is they have found a way to focus their efforts and not try to do everything all at once. These schools have learned to be proactive and to focus on one specific instructional area of the curriculum—an area that they consider to be the most important for their students to know and be able to do to be successful in life. Schools have chosen a wide variety of Instructional Focus areas, including literacy, reading comprehension, and critical thinking/problem solving.

It is important to note that an Instructional Focus is not simply a "focus on instruction." Instead, for school and central office staffs, it is the one thing they know and do excellently, expertly, better than anyone else, and in every classroom, every day, for every student.

- **An Instructional Focus is based on every student's learning needs as evidenced by multiple sources of data that has been disaggregated by various student groups.**

The critical activity in choosing an Instructional Focus is to examine data to identify student strengths, weaknesses, trends, and needs. Compile plenty of data from a variety of sources to create a clear picture of what students already do and do not know. At a minimum, this data should include standardized test results, local measures, and samples of student work. Disaggregate the data and examine it for patterns within or across different groups, such as by gender, race, and primary language.

Discuss this data with your staff. The emphasis of this conversation should be on continuous improvement rather than blame for current performance. We strongly recommend using a structured process to frame the discussion and encourage objective reflection rather than defensive reaction to this type of data. Suggestions for such specific processes are noted in the "Tools" section at the end of this chapter.

General questions to consider include the following:

- What does this data tell us about our students' current performance? In what curriculum areas are we the most successful? In what areas are we the least successful?
- What trends do we see over time?
- What patterns emerge from the disaggregated data?

Finally, examine the implications of your findings. Key questions to consider include these:

- Based on our students' performance, what is the one instructional area of the curriculum our students most need to improve upon?
- What instructional area is most important for our students to master?

After examining and discussing the implications of the data, choose an Instructional Focus that is based on a careful examination of the data and which relates to all students and connects directly to their identified needs. It is important to note that in our experience, deciding upon a focus takes time—at least a few months. Make sure to build in time and have patience to let the process run its course.

- **An Instructional Focus touches the whole school—every professional, every classroom, every day.**

Once the focus is selected, it will drive everything that happens at the school. Therefore, the entire school community—from principals, teachers, students, and secretaries to custodial, dining, and transportation staff—should be able to see him or herself in the focus. Early conversations must involve each faculty and support staff member to clearly identify how they contribute to the Instructional Focus. All students, regardless of their special needs, must be able to see themselves in the central core of the school's life. This is true for all special-needs students—at both ends of the spectrum—and for all classes all students take.

- **The principal and staff hold each other mutually accountable and expect every student to show growth in the area of the Instructional Focus. Any excuses for low performance based on race, gender, ethnicity, primary language, socio-economic level or class factors are *unacceptable*.**

Within the focus area, the principal and staff hold each other mutually accountable to do whatever it takes to assure that all students are successful. This usually means opening up classroom practice so that leadership and peers are continually visiting classrooms and meeting in grade-level or discipline teams to discuss instructional practice and data that shows the impact of that practice on student learning. It is not about "gotcha" types of evaluation but about supportive collaboration based on recognition that we all need to be involved in continuous improvement to meet the challenging goal of success for every student.

We have increasing evidence that almost all students are capable of mastering anything we teach in K-12. When a school selects a focus, it is expected that all resources will be applied to assure each and every student, with very few exceptions, is successful in that focus. This may be achieved by doing whatever it takes. Some students may require extra time—before school, after school, on weekends, or during double instructional periods. Some students may require smaller groupings or individual tutoring; some students may require special materials or instructional strategies and scaffolding.

GETTING STARTED

Two of the first things schools should do with their staffs to begin developing an Instructional Focus are to

- **build support for the Instructional Focus and**
- **examine their expectations of students.**

These steps both impact beliefs, and beliefs are directly connected to willingness to change.

- **Building Support for Instructional Focus**

As with all improvement efforts, it is essential to build staff support for the development and implementation of an Instructional Focus. In fact, the process for building this support is absolutely key to all other areas of the framework, for if the staff does not believe in this work, it will not translate into changes in teaching and learning. Undertaking this process—although time consuming and sometimes frustrating— is often the powerful lever by which staffs identify a need and execute a strategy to address that specific need. In our experience, staffs have found this process to be invaluable.

Below, you may see how one savvy principal and lead teacher helped build not only support but enthusiasm for changes in practice around the chosen Instructional Focus.

STORIES FROM THE FIELD:
Reviewing Data to Build Support for Instructional Focus

The principal and lead teacher of the Satoo Elementary School encouraged its staff to choose an Instructional Focus by using data to identify the urgent needs of the school's students. Concerned about slowly declining reading test scores, the principal raised the issue with her faculty at the first staff meeting of the year. The faculty responded that the decline was due to the fact that the students now enrolling in their school were just "not as smart as they used to be."

This sentiment created a sense of urgency in the principal's mind. She knew she had good students from good families with good teachers. It appeared the school and its staff was comfortable with being good enough—and this was something the principal was NOT comfortable with herself.

Working with her lead teacher, the principal realized that the faculty needed to learn how to change practice in order to change results. They wanted to find a way to help the staff see the urgency of the need for change, target professional development, and start discussions on evidence-based practices. They predicted roadblocks and reluctant staff members and thought through ways to help their teachers to see this process as a better way to do things, not just another way.

First, to address the realistic time constraints on staff, the lead teacher and principal decided to use substitute teachers and hold all in-services during the day—on "company time." A second process they thought would build support from the staff was to begin putting everything through the "Instructional Focus Funnel." If a school activity did not support the Instructional Focus, then it was not worth doing. Third, the team planned to pitch the idea of Instructional Focus not as a "new strategy" but as a way to bring focus to the work of teaching and learning. The principal knew if she could promise her teachers more time for teaching and less time for "other duties assigned," they would have more of a chance to focus on instruction and impact student learning.

> *At the August staff meeting, the lead teacher and principal led the staff in an activity suggested by Focus on Results to bring a sense of urgency and change to the faculty. The faculty created a Venn Diagram that identified the answers to the following questions: "What do our students need to know and be able to do to be successful? In what areas do our students need to improve?"*
>
> *The principal was surprised by the look of apprehension as the staff asked, "Don't you think we are already working as hard as we can?" Acknowledging the concerns and determined efforts by her staff, the principal realized she would need to work harder to build staff support before they could choose an Instructional Focus. She and her lead teacher developed a two-tiered communication strategy. While the principal repeated her message of the need for change to meet student needs, the lead teacher talked with each colleague one-on-one to assure them the work would help improve student learning while fitting into the current work day.*
>
> *Although the teachers' reluctance was clear, the team continued to focus on the need for an Instructional Focus and build momentum for the idea. Over the next three months, the team did not let the concept slip away. The principal used the main staff bulletin board to post their Venn Diagram, their perceived need as gleaned from test results, and how these two pieces would tie into an Instructional Focus. She began to use monthly staff meetings to share the number of events and school functions that she turned down on their behalf so that they could focus on instruction. The principal needed them to see that she was willing to "bargain" with them to earn their support.*
>
> *By November, the staff began to see they were making progress already—a notion that generated excitement and more momentum for improvement.*

• **Examine your expectations of students**

When developing an Instructional Focus, it is important to talk about your expectations for students. As described above, choosing an

Instructional Focus means accepting accountability for the performance of each and every student. Any excuse for performance based on race, gender, ethnicity, primary language, socio-economic level or class are unacceptable.

Staffs must explore the question, "Do we really believe that ALL of these kids can learn everything we are trying to teach them?"

A powerful tool in helping teachers see what "these kids" are capable of—whoever "these kids" are—is to visit a high-performing school with a similar population to yours. We have seen such visits to be so powerful that they completely turned around a reluctant faculty and got them excited about the possibilities for change. While it is preferable for an entire faculty to visit other schools, such journeys can have strong impact even when a smaller leadership team of carefully selected faculty attends.

There are many sources by which to search for a high-performing school to visit: the National Middle Grades Forum has identified a number of schools around the country as "Schools to Watch," the Disney Learning Partnership selects a "Spotlight School" each year, Blue Ribbon Schools are often receptive to visits, local universities can often help with referrals, and the Internet offers enormous potential for selecting a visitation site. Many new publications, such as Carter's *No Excuses*, or the 90-90-90 Schools that Doug Reeves has been studying, also offer powerful perspectives demonstrating that some schools—with kids like ours—are being very successful with all of their students. These visits send a clear message that the problem is NOT the students.

Finally, Jeff Howard's work on "The Social Construct of Intelligence" at the Efficacy Institute in Lexington, Massachusetts, is a great way to deepen a faculty's thinking and stimulate some exciting conversations. Remember, "problems are our friends." The only way we can deal with tense issues is to put them out on the table in plain view and begin to talk about them.

STORIES FROM THE FIELD:
Examining Student Expectations

Dennis school is an elementary school of about five hundred students nestled in a dense urban commercial area in the Dorchester neighborhood of Boston. The staff was a hotbed of union strength with three union reps in the building. Most of the staff had taught there for many years. Some described the staff as "calcified."

The school was working on developing an Instructional Focus in literacy based on their review of data. Their data showed clear decline in reading and writing over the last several years. Many initially pointed to the fact that "we have a lot of in-and-out kids who don't stay here from K-5. That is why we aren't making any gains."

The principal and clever leadership team responded by disaggregating the data to identify ONLY the students who had been at the school from K-5. This news was even worse. The results showed that students who had been there over time lost ground every year. Upon reading that data at the staff meeting, a particularly blunt staff member pounded her hand on the table, exclaiming, "You mean the kids are getting dumber the longer they go here?"

The surprising data helped the school see that yes, they did need a schoolwide focus on literacy. Even though they were not sure what that would mean, the faculty now shared a sense of urgency. However, many staff members were resigned to the "fact" that "these kids" were doing the best they could. The staff wondered, How can we, with the limited resources of the school, affect "these kids"?

Soon after, the Dennis school was granted an opportunity to visit a school located in the lower east side of New York City that had a well-established Instructional Focus in literacy with a population far more challenging than the Dennis school. The principal and a cross-section of teachers went to visit. The principal was sure to include both veterans and new staff. Also, she smartly included staff that she thought might be most resistant to the concept of focus.

They arrived late in the day after students went home. The New York principal requested this time of arrival, as he wanted to teach his visitors how to "read this school." His challenge to them was that if the school was truly focused on literacy, they should be able to read the walls filled with student and teacher work at any time of day—and they could.

The visiting team toured halls alive with student work, rigorous writing, and a clear focus on the joys and importance of reading. Other disciplines such as art, math, and science had clearly been tied to the literacy focus. Rooms were print-rich environments overstuffed with classroom libraries and evidence of a clear and systemic approach to the teaching of reading. . . and the students were not even there.

The next day the team saw the school in full swing and was impressed by the level of rigor they saw in the rooms and the sheer volume of how many adults were working with kids. In conversation with the principal and staff, the Dennis school staff pressed them to explain how they got so many potentially "at risk" students doing such sound academic work and how they got so many adults working with kids.

The answer to both was remarkably simple and obviously linked. The principal explained how once they clearly realized that literacy was the focus; they rethought and reconfigured everyone's role to support the literacy focus. They didn't get any more money or resources. They just used what they had and focused it around their clear goal of improving reading and writing. This allowed them to focus more on instruction and support for the students. This extra time and support, along with systematic evidence-based literacy practices, allowed these students to soar.

The impact on the visiting team was visceral. They saw that through common sense, focus, and hard work, teachers and administrators could really transform their school—even with a greater disadvantaged student population than the Dennis school. The team realized that they had set their expectations for their students too low. This visit provided overwhelming evidence that using the student population as an excuse for low performance was unacceptable—for "these kids" could learn to high standards.

The staff returned to the Dennis school eager to share their findings, pictures, and examples of what they saw with the staff. Although some were skeptical, their ideas were allowed to see the light of day, mostly because it was coming from peers—peers the staff knew and trusted—and a principal the staff was starting to trust. Within one month of the visit, they had created a realignment of their school day, based on what had been learned in New York, and were ready to give it a dry run.

DISTRICT SUPPORT

In Richard Elmore's work, he describes the concept of schools and districts often being "loosely coupled." As an organization, classrooms and schools can be seen as a part of the same entity, yet distinctly individualistic in terms of focus, actions, and accountability to the whole. Schools and districts that embrace the concept of an Instructional Focus often make great strides at bringing the organization together into a more focused whole.

In some districts, due to overwhelming evidence in student-learning data, a districtwide Instructional Focus is established where every school shares the same academic area as its focus. This allows the district to focus its resources and help schools to work together on a common challenge. Districts help by organizing training for school leaders both in the process and content of leading the work. The central office should act as a customer service agent to schools, helping them access high-quality, job-embedded staff development around evidence-based instructional practices most aligned to the district's Instructional Focus.

Other districts expect each school to develop an Instructional Focus based on its local data and situation. In this case, the district will help by organizing training for school leaders both in the process and content of leading the work and holding the schools accountable for clear expectations for implementation. These districts work hard to provide schools with a wider variety of professional development that is aligned with the variety of Instructional Focus areas schools develop.

In either situation, districts develop expectations for implementation to help schools translate the training into concrete action. An example of districtwide expectations can be seen below.

Orange Unified
School Improvement Expectations
August through June

Instructional Focus
There is more obvious evidence that the school has a schoolwide Instructional Focus in literacy.

Teacher Collaboration Teams
There is scheduled time for teachers to get together to talk about student work, teacher assignments, and effective teaching strategies within the Instructional Focus. The principal participates in these meetings.

Internal Accountability
The school has set at least two schoolwide SMARTe goals in support of the district goals. One is around the SAT9 as an external measure. The other is around a local measure in literacy. A baseline for the local measure has been established, and there is a plan to monitor student learning growth throughout the year.

Instructional Leadership Team
The team meets at least twice a month and is beginning to provide schoolwide leadership around the Instructional Focus in literacy.

Principal as Instructional Leader
The principal has shown progress toward meeting the goal of spending 50 percent of the time in classrooms observing, demonstrating, modeling, and supporting effective teaching practices within the Instructional Focus in literacy.

District Office Support
The district office team will work to support schools around the school improvement expectations by providing leadership, coaching, support, supervision, and creative problem solving to ensure schools can demonstrate dramatic growth in student learning.

Whether the focus is districtwide or chosen by individual schools, in either situation, the power continues to rest in the ability to focus. Creating this focus is really only the first step. For this clear focus to begin to transform teaching and learning, other areas need to be addressed.

TOOL FOR LEADERS

The tool in figure 1 is used to identify an Instructional Focus and encourages the district or school leaders to approach the issue as a conversation that includes multiple stakeholders and addresses multiple perspectives. The tool includes three strategies to help faculties examine their current students, strategies, and in-house expertise so they may think through and identify an Instructional Focus.

First, districts and schools may review student performance data. This data should include both standardized and local, often more authentic, data. The data should be organized to show trends over time and to show performance within and between different groups of students. The use of data can help identify several areas of need fairly quickly, but it is not the only indicator that should be included in the conversation.

A second way of discussing what the focus should be is to use some form of Venn Diagram or other graphic organizer to identify the key elements of different curricula. For example, one system's data suggested low performance in both reading comprehension and math applications. Staff in the system began putting essential skills for each area into one of the circles and then put those skills that were in both circles into the central overlap in the Venn. It quickly became clear that their students were having difficulty solving word problems because they could not read with clear understanding. After extended conversation, their focus became reading with understanding in literature and content areas.

Finally, a very important part of the conversation after data and skills are surfaced is the expertise of the professional staff. Being sure to ask, "What sense do we make of this?" is a way to engage the experience, knowledge, and wisdom of those who will be doing the work and helps to avoid mistakes that can be caused by not fully understanding the cultural context or the history of a situation.

It is important for leaders to remember that this process is a conversation, not a vote. Identifying an Instructional Focus does not need to take a long time, but it should be allowed to take as long as it needs in order to engage everyone affected by the decision in the conversation. It does not need to be chosen by unanimous consent, but it does need to be chosen after an extended conversation where all voices are heard and carefully considered. Numerous schools and systems have found much of the value in having an Instructional Focus comes from the conversations that led up to its selection.

Figure 1.1

Developing an Instructional Focus

Remember it's a conversation, not a vote.

Things to Think About

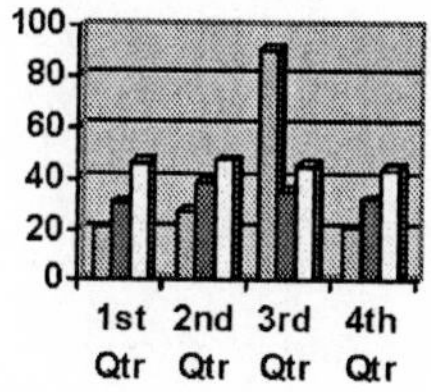

Data

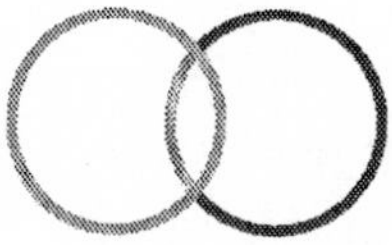

_____

_____

_____

_____

_____

Venn Diagram

_____

_____

_____

_____

Professional Experience

_____

_____

_____

_____

_____

Chapter 2

Area 2: Develop Professional Collaboration Teams to Improve Teaching and Learning for All Students

FOUNDATIONS

> **Area 2: Develop professional collaboration teams to improve teaching and learning for all students**
>
> - Every staff member joins a professional collaboration team that meets on a regular basis.
>
> - Professionals look at student work, teacher assignments, and student performance data in relation to the Instructional Focus and academic standards.
>
> - Based on its assessment of the data, the staff works to modify instruction, provide rigor, and create support systems to help all students meet high standards.
>
> - The staff learns to embrace diverse opinions.

- **Every staff member joins a professional collaboration team that meets on a regular basis.**

Why? The purpose of forming professional collaboration teams is to provide teachers with the time and tools they need to make instructional decisions based on their own students' data. Well-developed professional collaboration teams help by creating a trusted, safe environment for opening up the instructional practice of a school. These teams operate on the belief that all staffs are to be continuous learners in order to meet the challenging goal of success for every student.

Who? The structure of these teams varies greatly depending on local context. Some questions schools need to consider are: Should we build these teams with a mix of teachers and support staff, or separate them by function? Will we gain more benefit by mixing experienced and less experienced together, or by keeping new teachers in their own group? Should we create teams across departments or grade levels or within departments or grade levels? Does it matter how many are in each group? Who should determine our groups . . . administration, or teachers, or support staff?

From our perspective, all staff certificated to teach students, even if their current job description doesn't include teaching, should be involved in meeting on a regular basis with a consistent team of teachers to discuss issues pertaining to teaching and learning. Many uncredentialed staff can benefit from this process and many schools have found ways to engage parents in similar discussions.

It is very easy to develop tunnel vision when all you see and interact around is your own classroom or your own grade level or content area, yet to be most effective, a faculty needs to be able to view their individual roles as leaders within the larger school. Using a variety of groupings can sometimes help with this.

When? Our experience tells us that in order for professional collaboration teams to be truly successful, they must meet on a regular basis. The minimum meeting time is at least twice each month, for at least an hour each time.

It is essential that the time allotted to professional collaboration team meeting is used to its fullest potential. Limit the discussion to issues solely related to teaching and learning. Administrative issues, such as collecting information for reports, ordering texts, and planning next week's assembly should be handled at another time. Similarly, student study sessions, where only one student's educational need is the focus of the meeting, should be conducted separately.

How? Our experience shows that staffs who receive some training on how to function as a team get more value out of the professional collaboration teams and are able to function more effectively. Too often in education we try to "do" teams by fairy dust, hoping something magical will occur. Most teachers have spent the majority of their career operating in relative isolation in their own classrooms. It is foolish to think we can now put them around a table together, sprinkle a little fairy dust saying "Now collaborate, everyone," and expect it to work.

Teaching basic roles such as *facilitator, recorder, timekeeper, and process manager* and simple communication strategies such as *asking clarifying probing questions and giving warm and cool edible feedback* can make a big difference in helping the teacher teams become productive quickly.

- **Professionals look at student work, teacher assignments, and student performance data in relation to the Instructional Focus and academic standards.**

Professional collaboration teams must examine multiple sources of data to determine the strengths and weaknesses of both students and faculty. Teams should examine teacher assignments, samples of student work, and student performance data and discuss whether the work of both teachers and students supports the school's Instructional Focus and meets the academic standards.

For example, teams are encouraged to examine their classroom assignments and the resulting student work. (For details on strategies for looking at assignments, see the "Tool for Leaders" section of this chapter.) It is often the case that the better the assignment, the better the student work. The value of having a team reflect on these instructional issues is that we capture the combined experience of the members of the group. A school is much stronger when each person knows what everyone knows; teacher collaboration teams provide a process for this level of sharing to take place.

- **Based on its assessment of the data, the staff works to modify instruction, provide rigor, and create support systems to help all students meet high standards.**

This is, of course, the heart of the matter. By working together, teachers are able to share strategies that might work to address the needs shown in the data or student work. Einstein's definition of insanity was for someone to continue repeating the same action and expect to see a different result. It is only by changing what the students experience in the classroom that we can expect to see an improvement in their learning. This part of the collaboration process allows teachers to learn new approaches from each other, test them out in their classrooms, and revisit the data to measure the impact of their changes. Our schools will only be as effective as they can be when all of us know what each of us knows.

- **The staff learns to embrace diverse opinions.**

When teacher collaboration teams begin, we try to encourage them to listen first for understanding and then speak to be understood. We do not feel it is important to get agreement on all of the issues; even as to whether this paper was a three rather than a four. What seems to be far more valuable is learning to really listen to each other and to consider alternate perspectives and different possibilities.

It is important that the collaboration team sessions not be about "discussing to win." This is usually where someone puts one idea on the table; then someone else presents a different idea; and the rest of the time is spent taking sides until one of those ideas "win." Instead, this time is about learning to view instructional situations from new perspectives and gradually being willing to try new approaches in order to meet the needs of each of our students. We have found that providing specific, direct training in how to get along together and embrace diverse opinions is essential in maximizing the effectiveness of these teams.

GETTING STARTED

Two key strategies for launching a professional collaboration team are to

- **Build support for professional collaboration teams and**
- **Prevent these team meetings from becoming just another gripe session.**

- **Build Support for Professional Collaboration Teams**

Sharing the benefits. You are most likely to get "buy in" from teachers when two conditions are met: they can see some benefit to themselves in the change, and they have a say in shaping the change. Some of the benefits of collaboration teams at our schools have included

- getting help with challenging students,
- sharing assignments and reducing preparation time,
- participating in an exciting form of professional development—replacing boring presentations, and
- enhancing an individual teacher's sense of professionalism.

You can probably think of a number of benefits that fit your teachers' situation with whatever innovation you are implementing.

Create time for teachers to meet within the regular work day. The quickest way to kill "buy in" is if teachers see it as an add-on. Discuss with faculty what the professional collaboration team meetings will replace—what will you stop doing to make room for what you are starting to do. Carlene Murphy has a great article on finding time for faculty study groups that can offer clear suggestions. We have worked with thousands of schools over the past ten years, and never once has there been a school that wanted to have teacher collaboration teams but couldn't find the time; there's always a way. These collaborative conversations should be held during faculty meetings and professional development times as well as during team time to ensure many different perspectives are discussed.

STORIES FROM THE FIELD:
Looking at Student Work . . . With Food

A clever principal with the help of the school improvement coach wanted to find a way to make it easy for teachers to meet and collaborate. This large urban middle school set under the roaring flight path of jets bound for landing was known as a place where once the classroom doors shut, teachers "did their own thing." The relationship between the principal and the staff was cordial at best but more often veered off into struggles of power and control.

The district had set an expectation that all schools should provide the opportunity for teachers to collaborate on a regular basis, yet the question for this school was "when?" To meet this need, the principal created a schedule that combined each teacher's grade-level prep period with lunch. The combined amount of time was nearly ninety minutes. The principal was ecstatic at the thought of bimonthly ninety-minute sessions where teachers could collaborate and look at student work.

These collaboration sessions were "dead in the water" if the principal demanded everyone attend the entire ninety minutes, as forty-five of those minutes were a duty-free lunch. A few clever teachers advised the principal to create a way to meet that would honor the teachers' time and expertise. This team called it "Looking at Student Work . . . With Food."

The principal arranged for hot meals or sandwiches to be brought into the main meeting area which at this overcrowded school was the hallway outside the auditorium. Staff were invited to attend the lunch and expected to attend the "Looking at Student Work" part of the meeting.

When a few teachers inquired warily of the principal, "Are you saying we have to come to lunch? You know it's duty free?" The principal simply reminded them, "Of course not." They were welcome to stop by to join up for the lunch, but that was their choice, so long as they got there in time for the work session. The first month was tense. The smell of the steaming lasagna filled the auditorium foyer. The principal worried. Would anyone show? Many did. They ate, laughed and talked together for a bit, and before long they were ready to start the work session.

The "Looking at Student Work" session was productive. It was well facilitated and used a strong protocol. The teachers who attended saw value in the work, and they shared their positive experiences with others.

The next time, even more of the staff joined. By the third session, the entire staff was there and folks were wondering, "What's on the menu next time?"

- **Prevent these meetings from becoming just another gripe session.**

To prevent professional collaboration team meetings from becoming another gripe session, we suggest that you

- use a structured protocol for the meetings
- allow teachers to make decisions within given parameters
- follow up on staff recommendations and concerns

Use a structured protocol. When teachers meet, they need to have a structured protocol for their time. It is best to use an outside facilitator at first. Ensure this facilitator debriefs the team members on the strategies that he/she used, so the team will be able to assume facilitation of their own groups after four or five meetings. In addition, assign team members to be the recorder and timekeeper. To learn more about protocols, visit the Annenberg Institute for School Reform website at *www.studio.aisr.brown.edu* under the "Looking at Student Work" section. This site shares nine strong protocols, many of which may be adapted easily to fit specific needs or team preferences.

Allow teachers to make decisions. Ensure that team recommendations and decisions are shared throughout the school community. Principals must take care to share their thoughts, strategies, and plans as well—they often don't realize how much more information they have than classroom teachers. Many schools have a designated spot where teams post their minutes after each meeting. That way, other teams know what was discussed and can join in on recommendations or share strategies and resources that they have discussed in their meetings.

Follow up on staff recommendations and concerns. One important way to help teachers value these sessions is to be sure to follow up on decisions and recommendations made during their time together. If the principal attends the meetings or at least reads the minutes of each meeting, he/she can make fulfilling the requests and recommendations a priority with the goal to have everything accomplished; or at least provide an update on the status of each issue before the next meeting.

Nothing communicates the importance you place on these meetings more strongly than your follow-through. It doesn't necessarily mean the staff gets everything they ask for. However, the staff should get a response and an opportunity to dialogue about anything the faculty suggests will improve their teaching and their students' learning. Teachers then "own" the incremental improvements they have participated in shaping and the new practices are much more likely to become "the way we do things around here."

DISTRICT SUPPORT

Districts that are successful in building professional collaboration teams create an "expectation" that all schools develop opportunities to collaborate. For example, one district developed the following expectation for its schools.

> **Districtwide Expectation:** *Develop Professional Collaboration Teams to Improve Teaching and Learning.*
>
> *Using protocols and strategies, teacher teams meet regularly to talk about student work, teacher assignments, effective literacy practices, and data that demonstrate progress toward eliminating the achievement gap. The principal participates in these meetings. These meetings drive improvements in teaching and learning. The Instructional Leadership Team meets regularly and provides strong leadership around the schoolwide focus on literacy.*

Once the district sets up this expectation for all schools to support teachers in this manner, it must then follow through with support on many levels. For example, districts support schools by allowing them to be creative with timetables and bell schedules to create the teacher time. They support schools in finding ways to use resources differently to carve out time in the regular day for collaboration meetings. Often, if districts have minimum expectations for the amount of professional development a person is exposed to in a year, they include these teacher collaboration times as part of that. This sanctioning of time allows schools to solidify and legitimize this sound use of teachers' professional time.

In addition, the districts find ways to provide increased resources for schools around professional development and instructional support to ensure the content and conversation of the collaborative teams are rigorous ones. Districts often support the process of collaborative team development by providing training and mentoring in effective team development and, where possible, provide coaches and others to act as facilitators of school-based collaboration teams when needed.

Finally, when district offices model collaboration among their internal offices, they model for schools the power of collaboration. When schools see transportation and budget working together to support instruction and the Title I office working on a common district framework with the special education office, it sets an example for schools to open their practice and work as collaborative professionals with others.

TOOL FOR LEADERS

Collaboration around Assignments: Strategy and Protocol

As discussed, professional collaboration team meetings should examine multiple sources of data—teacher assignments, student work, and assessment data—to understand where the students and faculty are in relation to their goals and standards. This understanding of the current situation will help the faculty to make more informed decisions about how to change instruction to improve learning. The following tool describes in detail a process and protocol for discussing one of these data points—teacher assignments.

What Makes a Good Assignment? What Do Your Teachers Think?

Teachers give assignments to students every day and have some understanding about the quality of those assignments. However, when asked to think about a good assignment they had given recently, most teachers we have worked with judged quality based on the reaction of students to the assignment. We heard comments like, "My students really like this assignment. They were very engaged in the assignment and had lots of questions about it." Due to the fast-paced nature of most classrooms, teachers rarely reflected on what it was about the assignment that engaged the students. These assignments were often not developed by the teacher, but were part of the regular classroom curriculum, outlined in some teachers' manual. Even in this age of supposed standards-driven instruction, it seems that most assignments teachers give are still given "because that's the next page in the book."

Because teachers have this experience in regularly giving assignments, and because they seldom have time to reflect on the characteristics of those assignments, the Focus on Results approach begins by providing some sheltered time for teacher dialogue. We prefer to have teachers work in small groups of four or five, with several groups in the same room. These groups might be composed of grade-level/cross-grade articulation teams at elementary schools, or department/grade-level cluster teams at secondary schools. The grouping depends on the level of familiarity of the teachers with collaboration activities and the general level of trust in the school culture.

After a brief introduction about the importance of providing good assignments, each group is asked to talk together about what they think are the characteristics of good assignments. One person in each group serves as recorder to capture the group's thoughts. After about 15 minutes, the groups report what they know or think they know about the characteristics. These ideas are charted as they are presented. Usually, we accept one suggestion from each group in a round-robin fashion until all ideas have been charted. This often leads to a very powerful list, as it represents the combined experience and expertise of all teachers present. The list is then posted where all can see, and time is given for clarifying discussion of each of the characteristics listed. We are not lobbying for agreement at this point, just seeking to have consistent understanding.

The second step in the process engages the teachers in examining what others think about good assignments. For this we use both articles and examples. Using graphic organizers to help capture key ideas, each group is asked to read the articles and discuss the ideas presented to them. As part of the discussion, they are asked to compare the ideas in the articles with the characteristics posted on the charts, identifying those that the articles reinforce, those the articles present that are not listed on the charts, and those on the chart that are not presented in the articles.

After some whole-group discussion about those three comparisons, the group decides on any changes they want to make to the charts. This same process is then repeated using some example characteristics of quality assignments collected from other schools. This step concludes with consensus agreement on each of the characteristics of good assignments that remain on the charts, assuring participants the list will be revisited in about six months, after it has been used a few times by each team. The charts are then titled the "First Draft of Our School's Characteristics of Good Assignments." At this point, teachers are encouraged to go out and use this draft of characteristics as they design their lessons. In about two weeks, the teams come back for the third step.

The third step in this process is to introduce a simple "Making Good Assignments Protocol" and practice using it on a few sample assignments. Sample assignments are more objective and less threatening to teachers as they begin to open up their practice to inspection by others. The intent is for teacher teams to meet regularly to continue using the protocol as a precursor to learning and implementing a full "Looking At Student Work Protocol." A Facilitator Guide for each of these protocols is provided to participants, with simple steps such as these:

Making Good Assignments Protocol

Steps:

1. **Review Draft Characteristics (3 minutes):** The facilitator refers to the posted chart "Draft of Characteristics of Good Assignments" created by the staff. One team member reads the list aloud for the team.

2. **Presenting the Assignment (5 minutes):** The presenting teacher reads the assignment aloud to the team. It is helpful for the team to be able to see the assignment if possible. The presenting teacher gives a brief context for the assignment.

3. **Clarifying Questions (2 minutes):** The team members ask clarifying questions. The facilitator ensures the questions are clarifying and the presenting teacher answers quickly and succinctly.

4. **Characteristics That Match (5 minutes):** The team discusses ways the assignment matches the charted characteristics. The facilitator helps the team members provide specific evidence of the matching characteristics in this assignment.

5. **Probing Questions (5 minutes):** The team members focus on characteristics that may not be evident in this assignment by asking probing questions. The team members are seeking to understand the presenting teacher's thinking and to help expand their own thinking. The questions are open-ended.

6. **Deepening the Conversation (5 minutes):** The facilitator may introduce the following questions to deepen the conversation:

— Were the directions clear?
— Was the task or the problem clear?
— Did students know what they were expected to do?
— Did they have exemplars against which they could judge their work?
— Did the assignment match the skills and content the students should know?
— Did the assignment help students meet standards? Which standards? How?
— What are some other strategies we could use to teach this skill?

7. **Providing Feedback (5 minutes):** The facilitator guides the conversation so that the team gives feedback that is edible, credible and actionable, and so that the presenting teacher does not become defensive. Questions to consider are:

— What might make this a better assignment?
— What might the next assignment be?

8. Team members thank the presenting teacher and decide who will bring the next assignment.

Using this process with thousands of teachers has led to the identification of several characteristics of good assignments that are listed below. This is not the "right" list, but it may prove interesting to compare it to the list your teachers develop and to discuss similarities and differences.

The most frequently included characteristics of good assignments are:

- Connects to students' prior knowledge and builds on or extends it,
- Challenges students to use higher-order thinking skills,
- Engages the students' interests,
- Sets clear expectations of what good work looks like on the assignment,
- Allows a range of ways to communicate learning,
- Provides opportunity to reflect on work and revise after receiving feedback,
- Connects to standards, goals, and assessments,
- Provides the resources and support each student needs to be successful, and
- Is fun.

Taken together, these characteristics create a guide for powerful teaching. If every assignment, in every classroom, every day included all or most of these characteristics of "good assignments" we might be well on the way to seeing a dramatic increase in "good work" from our students. This won't just happen by itself, though. Intentional leadership is necessary to engage teachers in collaboratively identifying what characteristics of good assignments are, and in assuring the implementation of those characteristics on a regular basis through additional teacher collaboration opportunities and direct in-classroom observation and support.

Chapter 3

Area 3: Identify, Learn, and Use Effective Evidence-Based Teaching Practices To Meet the Needs of All Students.

FOUNDATIONS

Area 3: Identify, learn, and use effective evidence-based teaching practices to meet the needs of all students.

- Find effective evidence-based practices at school, in your district, and beyond.

- Select a small set of evidence-based teaching practices (three to five) that are tied to your Instructional Focus.

- Ensure the effective practices promote good teaching, model rigorous work, and meet the needs of a diverse student population.

- Develop a strategy for building expertise and ensuring change in practice.

It is amazing how much has been learned in the past thirty years about how the mind works. It is perhaps equally amazing how little of that knowledge has found its way into many classrooms.

Richard Elmore talks about the "loose coupling" of schools as being largely responsible for this. At many schools, once a teacher is inside their own classroom—often with the door closed—they are master of their curriculum. They alone decide, and in many cases they alone know, what gets taught and how it is delivered. Since most teachers work very hard for long hours each day, many are not able to keep up with the literature on effective teaching and instead stick to strategies they have used for years; often strategies they experienced as students. Breaking this cycle is essential. Only when schools move to the consistent use of evidence-based instructional practices does student learning accelerate dramatically.

There are several important points to consider about the identification and use of evidence-based teaching strategies.

- **Find effective evidence-based teaching strategies at school, in your district, and beyond.**

Schools do not need to rely solely on some research report to find practices they know will work with "our" students. Most schools could find teachers using effective practices under their own roofs. Taking a close look at student data classroom by classroom can highlight those practices that work best in any given setting. Visit those classrooms to observe the instructional practice used and consider how it might work for other teachers.

It is often a good idea to go beyond the local school and identify strong practitioners in the nearby geographical area who are getting excellent results in their schools. A staff often finds it easier to accept expertise when it comes from outside of their own closed culture.

Finally, it is our experience that when a certain set of practices work, it is almost always supported by the literature. Reading up on the background of strong practices is an excellent way to further identify the appropriate practices for a given school.

- **Select a small set of evidence-based teaching practices (three to five) that are tied to your Instructional Focus.**

This is sometimes difficult for schools to do. The students often have so many areas of low performance that schools want to master all of the related strategies yesterday. What we are talking about through this framework is a major shift in culture from unsupervised teacher selection of a wide range of instructional practices to a much more consistent use of a more narrow range of evidence-based practices. In order to facilitate this major shift, it is essential that only a few strategies be addressed at a time; which means, of course, that we select key strategies that will generate the best leverage for increasing student learning.

If writing across the curriculum were the focus at a middle school, for example, they might choose only three evidence-based practices such as the use of a particular five-step writing process, graphic organizers for prewriting, and rubrics for assessing growth. While this is a small set of strategies, it would require a very effective, targeted professional development plan to fully implement those three in every classroom.

- **Ensure the effective practices promote good teaching, model rigorous work, and meet the needs of a diverse student population.**

As strategies seem to emerge for a school, it is important to ensure that they meet these conditions for effectiveness. It is sometimes tempting to select strategies that are too simple or that won't require any real change in practice. This is where the review of the literature is so important. School leadership teams need to ask the hard questions: Is this practice supported by research? Do we believe it will lead to mastery of a rigorous curriculum? Is it appropriate for the diversity of our student population—is it something that will positively impact ALL of our students?

- **Develop a strategy for building expertise and ensuring change in practice.**

The identification of evidence-based teaching practices is a complete waste of time unless it is closely aligned to powerful professional development that builds true expertise in every teacher and is implemented in every classroom, every day, for every student. Einstein's definition of insanity was to do the same thing over and over while expecting to get a different result. The only way we can expect to see a dramatic improvement in student learning is when we see a similarly dramatic change in instructional practice.

STORIES FROM THE FIELD:
Using "Best Used Reading Practices" (BURPs)

Satoo located in a large urban system, began the school year by identifying an Instructional Focus. After great anxiety, reluctance, and a list of excuses, the staff identified reading comprehension as its schoolwide focus. While this was a great feat in itself, it was now upon the school to find a small set of effective, evidence-based teaching practices that could translate this focus into improvement for students.

With this in mind, the principal hired a reading consultant to work with the staff for five months on comprehension issues. She made sure that these sessions were scheduled during school time as to not add more work to the faculty's already full plate. The more the consultant discussed reading in general, the more the faculty realized they did not know a great deal about reading comprehension. The staff became energized and interested, and the principal was cautiously optimistic.

As this first year progressed, the staff worked through challenges around looking at student work, writing lesson plans, and dealing with information overload from the reading consultant. The principal made

---

clear that staff were expected to implement the strategies they learned every day with every student to ensure the professional development translated into changes in teaching and learning.

By May, the teachers were nervous about the district reading tests, but the principal was confident they would improve. And did they improve! Results rose in all grades including a 25 percent increase in students reading at grade level from grade five to grade six. These were the same students the faculty had claimed "were just not as 'smart' as they used to be." The principal held a debriefing session at the next staff meeting, thinking the staff would be pleased with the results. Although they were happy, they were more worried about carrying the momentum into the next year wondering, "Could we do it again?"

To address these concerns, the faculty used their next professional development session to identify a small number of schoolwide evidence-based practices they had learned from their work with the consultant. The Instructional Leadership Team posted these practices in the staff room to reinforce them and help the faculty remember what good work looked like as they prepared for the upcoming year.

When the next school year began, the faculty revisited this list of practices they had learned and worked to translate it into a concrete set of practices everyone could all articulate and use. As the discussion progressed, the faculty coined the phrase BURPs, "Best Used Reading Practices," to represent their small set of evidence-based practices. BURPS ended up being a masterful stroke. It turned the small set of evidence-based practices into a fun, user-friendly term that teachers, parents, and most importantly, students could understand. It moved the implementation and accountability for actually using the evidence-based practices into a community responsibility. Was it possible this Focus work may even be fun?

They set the goal for the year to implement as many BURPs as possible into as many different subjects as possible to try and find the very best of the best.

> *BURPs paid off for students. After using BURPs for two years, the students demonstrated an average increase of twenty points in their reading results.*

GETTING STARTED

• **What is the difference between a practice, a method, or a model?**

Sometimes schools get caught up in trying to find the perfect evidence-based practice or in arguing over whether a certain practice is actually more a method or model of teaching. Semantics are less important here than common sense. Selecting the best instructional practices to address your students' needs and help you meet your goals is usually achieved using a combination of observation, reading, and teacher expertise.

Observing classrooms where teachers are getting good results with all students and reading about approaches that are working well with "kids like ours" helps to identify certain things teachers can do or certain ways classrooms can be organized to promote higher learning levels. When all staff agrees on a small set of teaching practices, student success often stems not from the strategies alone, but also from the consistency of their experience across classrooms.

Some schools we work with have identified Resnik's "Principles of Learning" as a framework on which to focus evidence-based practices. Other schools have chosen a particular questioning strategy, like the "Socratic Method," they all master and then implement in daily instruction. Some schools select a five or seven step writing process with a common rubric that they believe will enhance the writing of their students.

Each of these approaches is fine, as long as it meets certain criteria, which include the following:

• connected to the focus,

- reflects student needs as indicated by a range of data,
- combined with a targeted professional development plan that builds true expertise in the practice for every teacher, and
- is implemented in every classroom, every day, for every student, with ongoing adjustment based on frequent monitoring of student learning data.

DISTRICT SUPPORT

Here is where districts are invaluable to schools. Districts can help schools to identify and use these high potential practices by providing professional development in schools' areas of interest. Central office instructional support staff must provide rich resources and timely and ongoing job-embedded staff development to help faculties investigate and determine appropriate practices.

Many districts work hard to arrange opportunities for effective teachers to showcase their work. Some examples of this include school best practice days, organized school inter-visitations, and the establishment of observation classrooms where other teachers may visit and see particular practices being well implemented.

The key is for the district not simply to tell schools to "pick your practices from this list" but to create a true and supporting professional learning community where the district acts as a supportive and effective coach. The district coaching around best practice selection should help the school not only reach their own decisions about the practices but select practices that are rigorous and evidence-based. Some districts develop "critical attributes" of what makes a good best practice and use those attributes as a teaching tool to help schools make wise decisions.

TOOL FOR LEADERS

Although each school follows its own unique path, there are some common elements to the approaches schools take to identify their evidence-based practices. The graphic below outlines the cycle of questions and actions schools take to get started. Faculties or Instructional Leadership Teams may use this chart to focus discussion on identifying targeted, effective teaching practices. Each discussion might be a month to six weeks apart, with time to implement that part of the plan between meetings. The value of the cycle is in showing that this is not a one-time decision, but an ongoing discussion with the goal of continuous improvement.

Figure 3.1

Cycle of Discussion and Questioning for Identifying Best Practices

4. Sharing and Teacher Collaboration and Learning Teams
- How are we supporting one another to implement the practice?
- What information are we getting from the student work?
- What specific knowledge or instructional skills do teachers need in order to adapt the practice?

1. Potential New Evidence-Based Practice
- Does it support, replace, or extend the other evidence-based practices in the school?
- Does it meet the critical attributes?
- The potential evidence-based practice will help with . . .
- Who can try it out?

3. Experiment
- How will this practice look in individual classrooms and in the whole school?
- What evidence will we accept that the practice is having an impact?

2. Professional Development
- What do we need to learn about this practice?
- In what format will we learn what we need? (Targeted Professional Development, study group, etc.)
- What internal expertise do we have?
- How can we see them using it?

Adapted from Curriculum Training Materials developed by Tanni Parker, Edmonton Public Schools, 2004.

Chapter 4

Area 4: Create a Targeted Professional Development Plan that Builds Expertise in Selected Evidence-Based Practices.

FOUNDATIONS

Area 4: Create a targeted professional development plan that builds expertise in selected evidence-based practices.

- The plan is coordinated around the small set of identified practices, tied to the Instructional Focus, and linked to results for all students.

- It is site-based, ongoing, and includes frequent opportunities for practice and coaching.

- The district acts as a customer service provider to meet school professional development needs.

- The professional development plan builds true expertise as well as ensures change in practice.

- Effectiveness is measured by significant growth in student learning and the closing of any achievement gap.

Almost everyone involved in education for more than a few years is subjected to the typical poor-quality professional development practiced in so many districts. It is too often delivered in adult-unfriendly environments, involving some "expert" who often isn't, talking at teachers about something too esoteric to actually use in their classroom. Occasionally, one is also fortunate enough to be able to participate in quality professional development, such as with The National Writing Project, three-week Math and Science institutes offered in the summers by different universities, or the Lit Conn training for working with English Language Learners.

The difference between typical and quality is staggering. Huge amounts of money are spent annually by many, many districts with no indication of change in teacher behavior. To improve student learning, targeted, quality professional development must build true expertise and help teachers actually use the training in regular classroom instruction on a daily basis.

There are five key concepts to consider when developing this targeted professional development plan.

• **The plan is coordinated around the small set of identified practices, tied to the Instructional Focus, and linked to results for all students.**

Targeted professional development means that every single session offered throughout the year is connected directly to the schoolwide Instructional Focus and the small set of evidence-based practices the school has selected. The purpose of the professional development is to build the capacity of all teachers in these evidence-based practices in order to be able to meet the SMARTe Goals (specific, measurable, attainable, relevant, time-bound, and touch every student) the school has set for itself in the area of the Instructional Focus. In a high school with an Instructional Focus on reading comprehension, all professional development for the mathematics department would be connected to how to teach math vocabulary, use word problems, engage students in oral and written explanations of how they solved their problems, etcetera. This would not be the time to offer a three-day workshop on how to program calculators—unless doing so was directly connected to the evidence-based practices the school had selected.

- **It is site-based, ongoing, and includes frequent opportunities for practice and coaching.**

Targeted professional development that just sends a few people off to workshops has never worked very well. Changing instructional practice in any broad way requires the culture of the school to change.

This is best accomplished when the professional development is site based and the entire staff—including the principal and other non-classroom personnel—is engaged in the training at the same time. As Roland Barth says, "You can't lead where you won't go." When school leaders and administrators know the new strategies as well as teachers, they are all new learners together, sharing new vocabulary, experimenting with new strategies, and communicating from equal footing.

Such sessions should also include frequent opportunities for practice and coaching. It is much easier to experiment with the practices and accept feedback from others if everyone on the staff is experiencing the same situation.

- **The district acts as a customer service provider to meet school professional development needs.**

District staff need to think of themselves as a customer service organization that does anything it takes to support its clients—the schools. Traditional central offices are not focused in this way and often offer professional development that is uncoordinated across district content areas, competes with professional development linked to the school's SMARTe Goals, and is disconnected to the school's actual needs.

When the whole district has the same focus, such as literacy, it is easier for districts and their content specialists to tailor their training to support the schools. When schools have different areas of focus, it is essential that the central system respect and support the schoolwide, site-based professional development and not compete with it. In some cases, this may require a restructuring of central services.

- **The professional development plan builds true expertise as well as ensures change in practice.**

Too much professional development in the past is simply exposure to key concepts or good strategies. What is needed is a comprehensive approach that differentiates training by individual teacher needs and encourages the development of true expertise. The plan should allow for a range of input opportunities and structures that leads all teachers to truly be masters at the use and delivery of the intended instructional practices.

Along with, and equally important to high-quality training, is the implementation of strategies to ensure the training leads to actual change in practice in every classroom. Schoolwide walkthroughs serve this purpose and enable principals and leadership teams to collect data on the implementation of new strategies in the classrooms. This data may then inform decisions about professional development and resource allocation.

A second strategy to ensure change in practice is for principals to be in classrooms or working with teachers on instructional issues at least 50 percent of each day. Opening up the school culture to the point where teachers expect frequent visits by others and are given the opportunity to frequently visit other classrooms is the only sure way to build continuous change of practice into a school culture.

- **Effectiveness is measured by significant growth in student learning and the closing of any achievement gap.**

Participants should have the opportunity to provide feedback for every professional development activity by sharing how well it was presented and connected to their learning needs. This can help continuously improve future training sessions.

The ultimate evaluation of the effectiveness of any professional development program, however, is not how entertaining the sessions were, but whether or not the sessions have led to an increase in student learning. Part of any good professional development program is a way to collect and review data on how the new strategies impact student achievement. This is typically the work of the Instructional Leadership Team, but it impacts the whole school. Adjustments to the training should be made regularly based on student data and teacher discussion about the implications of the data.

GETTING STARTED

- **Elements of a strong targeted professional development plan.**

Strong, targeted professional development is for the entire school or district. It is site-based, ongoing (at least six times per year) with practice, coaching, and demonstration lessons between each session. It also includes continuous circulation of articles relating to a clear school or districtwide focus.

The following four strategies are critical elements of a successful, targeted professional development plan.

Figure 4.1

Critical Elements of a Targeted Professional Plan: The Four Strategies

Targeted professional development plans must achieve the following:

Build expertise | **Help folks know what to do.**
A yearlong professional development plan should be differentiated, site-based, and include coaching and peer visits.

Change Practice | **Hold each other accountable for doing it.**
School staff should hold each other mutually accountable through regular visitations, classroom walk-throughs, and formal and informal observation by the principal and others.

Monitor Student Performance | **Chart the impact on student performance.**
Growing out of our SMARTe targets (specific, measurable, attainable and challenging, relevant, time-bound, and touch every student) staffs should regularly assess all students (every six to eight weeks) using an internal measure; then review, share, and post the data publicly.

Communicate Relentlessly | **Always talk about what you are doing.**
Share updates and information about this work through staff and team meetings, weekly bulletins, e-mail, and all other school communication vehicles.

Schools and districts should ensure that professional development plans are solid and address all four strategies above. The strategies serve distinct purposes so that when taken together, they help faculties define a clear, cohesive, and specific plan to ensure professional development turns into improved classroom practice.

• **Principals spend 50 percent of their time in classrooms.**

The best way to be sure there is actually a change in classroom practice is for teachers to know that people will be coming in and out of their classrooms frequently to observe the new practices. It is essential that the principal be a part of this; teachers know what the principal values by how he/she spends time. If they know the principal is going to be in and out often, looking for evidence of the new practices, they are much more likely to begin using them—especially if it is clear that all faculty are all experimenting with the strategies and the principal is there to help them— not as their evaluator. Teachers are also less threatened when they know exactly what observers are looking for—the new practice the way everyone learned it. This is why it is important for teachers to see principals receiving the training with them and even practicing the new approaches in different classrooms in order to build everyone's expertise.

The principal should not be the only person going into classrooms to observe. It is important the teachers themselves are able to observe each other implementing new practices. One rule of thumb we have used is that every non-classroom teacher is expected to take over classrooms for teachers at least two hours per week—usually in half hour increments— so all teachers can spend at least thirty minutes per week observing other teachers. When we talk about the principal being in classrooms 50 percent of each day, this is one of the ways we suggest the principal spend that time—taking over for teachers to observe. The principal and specialists in the area of focus (the Reading Teacher if the focus is literacy) should also be in classrooms doing demonstration lessons, and team teaching as teachers try out new strategies.

Fifty percent of each day may seem unrealistic at first, but it is actually quite doable, and lots of principals have found ways to make it happen. The principal does not need to start with that much, though. It's okay to start slowly—an hour and a half or two hours per day at first. Either way, be sure to inform the teachers, the community, and central office about what is being done and why. They need to know in advance why they can't find the principal at their convenience. It is also crucial that the principal not do unnecessary paperwork—delegate when possible, wait for the third phone call on some of it, and work with other principals to help your central office find alternative ways to get information. This cannot be an add-on for you—it is too important. It must replace business as usual, and take on this new fundamental role.

One strategy that may help principals spend more time in classrooms is to change how the discipline is handled. Schools that have minimal discipline issues combine a set of clear, schoolwide expectations with engaging instructional practice. Students must see that teachers have authority too, and students should not see the principal for behavioral infractions until teachers have handled several steps themselves first— including contacting parents.

One school saw a sharp decline in discipline issues when they combined a new student-centered curriculum with a specific behavior plan that included putting phones in each classroom (no incoming calls to interrupt.) Teachers were expected to call at least three families each afternoon to leave positive messages, as well as messages concerning any students who needed to improve.

DISTRICT SUPPORT

Districts may support this work in many different ways, depending on the individual culture and conditions of the district. However, one concept remains as a constant: **The district must act as a customer service provider to meet school professional development needs.**

This happens in several ways. For example, some districts have allowed schools to create menu-driven professional development based on cafeteria-style offerings. In these districts, one of the best places to start is to create a clear expectation that ALL schools will create a targeted professional development plan and provide school teams with training to achieve this goal.

For example, one district set their professional development plan expectations as follows: "The school's professional development supports the focus on literacy by building teacher expertise and promoting high expectations for all students. As expertise is developed, teachers are held increasingly accountable for implementation of strategies."

Once the expectation is set, the district must provide schools with training and easy-to-use templates and tools to help school leaders develop those plans. Beyond setting these expectations, "customer service" can look quite different depending on the local culture of the district. Some districts may simply realign their resources to ensure the professional development offerings actually match the areas of identified need. Others determine a districtwide focus, such as literacy, and ensure it provides strong professional development to support that focus.

For example, schools in New Bedford, Massachusetts identified writing as their Instructional Focus. To ensure the district met schools' professional development needs in this area, they provided each school with a centrally-funded content coach. Each coach received the same training in the subject, and in turn, conducted on-site demonstration lessons to ensure the teachers developed writing expertise and changed their practice.

In Edmonton, Alberta where each school sets its own focus, they centrally organized a fee for service consultant core and totally revamped all their professional development offerings to make sure they more clearly met the needs of the 207 schools. They hired and retrained their consultant core and created a specific strand of work to support secondary literacy, all in an effort to make sure they were centrally meeting the customer needs of their client schools.

STORIES FROM THE FIELD:
Targeted Professional Development at Prospect Produces Results

Prospect Elementary is a medium sized K-6 school located in a diverse urban district in Orange, California. The school has nearly 50 percent of its students on Free and Reduced Lunch and one fourth of its students are considered English Language Learners.

With the support of a new principal and strong leadership team, the staff identified an Instructional Focus in literacy and worked hard to create a targeted professional development plan tied to this focus. First, they developed a calendar that outlined all professional development

activities to take place over the entire school year. As the leadership team planned the year, they carefully selected activities that were true to their Instructional Focus in literacy, supported a small set of evidence-based teaching practices, and addressed the four strategies (Build Expertise, Change Practice, Monitor Impact on Student Learning, and Communicate Relentlessly).

See the figures below to get a better picture of their planning.

Figure 4.2

	Sept.	Oct.	Nov.	Dec.	Jan.	Feb.	Mar.	Apr.	May	June
Build Expertise										
Project Read	X-12									
Rec. of Rd. Behavior	12									
Strategy Reading		10								
Center Ideas		17								
Interactive Writing			1							
Modeled				5						
Writing/Grammar										
Rdg. Comp./Fluency					16					
Word Wall/Making						13				
Words										
Shared Reading							27			
Staff-development Day							13			
Ensure Change in Practice										
Bldg. Walk Through-teacher			13,14,15			26.27,28			7,8,9	
Writing Sample Discussion	3					26				7
Monitor Impact on Student Learning										
Writing Samples		3			23				29	
San Diego Quick	X				X				X	
Student Work Samples			X	X	X	X	X	X		
Communicate, Monitor, and Adjust										
Rec. of Rd. Behavior	26									
Strategy Reading		24								
Center Ideas			15							
Interactive Writing				19						
Modeled					30					
Writing/Grammar										
Rdg. Comp./Fluency						27				
Word Wall/Making								11		
Words										
Shared Reading										
Staff-development Day										

After planning the dates for each professional development event over the year, the team took the plan to the next level by detailing how each professional development activity in the targeted plan would actually be carried out. The plan clearly reflected accountability and responsibility and was organized in a way that people actually used to drive real improvement in instruction and learning. Below, see Prospect's professional development plan for the month of September.

Figure 4.3

	Date	Who's Involved	Where	Who's Responsible	Funding	District-office Support
Build Expertise						
Project Read	12	Teachers	Library	M. Paul	Title 1	
Phonemic Awareness	20	Teachers	Rm. 12	M. Bielat, C. Burns	Title 1	
Rec. of Rdg. Beh.—fluency Test	26	Teachers	Rm. 10	A. Gutierrez, C. Burns	Title 1	
Ensure Change in Practice						
Proj. Read—follow-up		Staff-trained	Classrooms	Principal		
Leadership Team Meeting	9	Team	Rm. 21	Principal		
Monitor Impact on Student Learning						
Writing Sample	19	All Students	Prospect	Staff/Principal		
District Rubric	19	Staff	Library	Staff/Principal/DO Assess.		
Communicate, Monitor, and Adjust						
Rec. of Rdg. Beh.—fluency Test	4-Oct	Teachers	Rm. 10	A. Gutierrez, C. Burns	Title 1	
Phonemic Awareness	4-Oct	Teachers	Rm. 10	M. Bielat, C. Burns	Title 1	

The Instructional Focus and reflecting targeted professional development plan paid off for the students and teachers at Prospect Elementary. The students demonstrated impressive gains in student achievement and improved in literacy by eighty three total points on Academic Performance Indicators and 6.5 NCE points on the Total Reading score.

TOOL FOR LEADERS

One helpful strategy for creating a targeted Professional Development Plan is to compare school's or district's current plans to other professional development plans to identify the strengths and weaknesses in your own plan.

Use the Discussion Guide below to lead your team through this valuable activity.

Five Professional Development Examples
Graphic Organizer
Questions for discussion

First, compare Your Professional Development Plan with each of the Five Examples below. Read each example and work with a partner or at your table group to compare what we know about solid professional development and the examples. Then work together to compare the strengths of each example to your own Professional Development Plan. Where do you see connections? What's missing?

FIVE EXAMPLES of PROFESSIONAL DEVELOPMENT PLANS

Example 1: Building Expertise
Three-Year to Expert Plan

1. Principal or leadership team negotiates an area of expertise to be developed by each staff member. Areas negotiated are based on student needs and individual staff talent or interest. There is usually more than one person in each area. Each area is directly connected to the school's focus (e.g., school focus = literacy. Some staff members become experts in Writing Strategies in Investigation-based Science).

2. Expert is defined as "knowing as much about this area as anyone in the country."

3. A three-year plan is designed and implemented for building expertise.

4. Year 1: Staff Member

    Joins local and national organization in that area
    Identifies books and articles to be read and discussed
    Attends conference in that area

Identifies a few strategies to experiment with in his or her classroom, measuring impact on student learning
Presents periodic updates to total staff
Provides summary report of findings at end of year

Year 2: Staff Member

Continues all of the above
Provides observation opportunities of effective practices
Presents workshop on effective practices for staff
Is videotaped monthly—for self-review

Year 3: Staff Member

Continues all of the above
Provides demonstration lessons of effective practices
Presents workshop for district, area, or state conference
Produces video of series of lessons for others to view
Publishes article
Assumes leadership role at district, area, or state level

*   *   *

Example 2: Building Expertise
Districtwide Coaching Model

1. District identifies single Instructional Focus and sets SMARTe Goals for that area.

2. District reallocates resources (Title I, grants, etcetera.) to support at least one "specialist" or "coach" in the area of the focus at each school. District then identifies or hires qualified personnel and assigns them to each school.

3. District identifies evidence-based practices in area of focus and trains all coaches in those practices and in coaching and training techniques—including assessment and data-review strategies.

4. District also trains principals in evidence-based practices and coaching techniques.

5. Coaches provide training for staff members at their schools, including follow-up demonstration lessons, and observation feedback.

6. Coaches also serve as facilitators by organizing instructional and assessment materials and facilitating teacher study and Looking at Student Work groups.

7. Principals work with coaches to deliver training, monitor implementation, and review assessment data with teachers.

8. Coaches from all schools meet weekly to share successes, challenges, new understandings, and to continue their own training.

*   *   *

Example 3: Building Expertise
Single Best Practice Example

1. Through a series of faculty discussions and an examination of student work and performance data, the faculty identifies a specific area of student need—e.g., it was determined that students needed more support around how to have disciplined, thoughtful, and intellectually challenging conversations.

2. Several teachers, with the support of the school leadership team, decide to investigate a specific best practice—e.g., Socratic Seminar—as a possible schoolwide strategy to address this need.

3. School teams visit schools that have implemented the strategy schoolwide and attend local or national conferences focused on

using that best practice—Socratic Seminar—as a schoolwide improvement strategy.

4. Implementation: Through careful conversation and reports back to teachers, the staff decides to move ahead with the best practice, with the following ground rules:

- Everyone on staff (principals, counselor, librarian, etc.) will be expected to participate.
- Staff will receive ongoing training, not a one-shot day in the fall.
- Staff will be given time to work together and learn together during implementation.
- Staff will not be "formally evaluated" during their attempts to deliver a Socratic Seminar in the first year.
- Staff will be able to reevaluate at the end of the year, based on student achievement results.

*   *   *

Example 4: Building Expertise
Curriculum Mapping Process

1. The school examines multiple sources of data to determine an area of Instructional Focus: Reading Comprehension.
2. Led by the principal and teacher leaders, the school spends time reading and learning about the components of Reading Comprehension during team and faculty meetings.
3. Under the direction of the teacher leaders, the school identifies essential components of the focus (i.e., main idea, sequencing.)
4. During several months teachers take time to "map" where these essential components are supported, in their curriculum and aligned with their external assessments. They also outline specific instructional support materials (texts, supplemental materials, etc.) to be used with each essential component.

5. The Instructional Leadership Team (ILT) creates a map for the academic year that outlines when and how the essential components will be articulated throughout the year. This map follows a simple pattern that is repeated monthly:

   a. Professional Development for staff in the essential component.
   b. Pretest for all students in the essential component.
   c. Teacher support and coaching in lesson design around the essential component.
   d. Looking At Student Work session focusing on assignments and student work products around the essential component.
   e. Post-test for all students in the essential component.
   f. All school meeting to reflect on results of data from assessments as well as looking at work and assignment sessions.

*   *   *

Example 5: Building Expertise
Intensive, Content-Specific Design

1. Within a particular content area, principal and staff examine student achievement data (performance assessments, standardized test scores, Looking at Student Work) to identify two or three areas of focus based on student needs—i.e., problem solving, understanding algebraic concepts.
2. Principal and staff identify an initial cohort of teachers (by either grade-levels or content area) to participate in content area professional development.
3. Identified staff participates in intensive initial two-week training in evidence—based instructional approach that addresses identified student needs—i.e., experiential learning model.
4. Designated staff participates in bi-weekly/monthly colleague

dialogue groups to discuss and refine implementation of the identified pedagogical model in the content area. Identified content specialist (either school or district based) or other identified point person, trained in the model serves as facilitator during the early meetings. As meetings progress and relationships build, identified teachers participate in peer visits and videotaping sessions to continually improve practice.

5. Each participating teacher also receives regular coaching visits from content specialist or support contact trained in the pedagogical approach and knowledge in the content-area (first year of implementation—two to three times per month; second year of implementation—one to two times per month). Coaching includes demonstration lessons, pair teaching and informal observation and feedback.

6. Teachers in both the first and second year of implementation participate in content-specific professional development sessions (at least five times per school year) that reflect identified student needs. These professional development sessions are designed to engage teachers in advanced content topics using techniques that reflect the identified pedagogical model.

7. Teachers are supported through at least two years of implementation. Teachers further along in the professional development cycle provide information and training to the larger staff—i.e., teachers from different content areas who may support student learning in the focus content area.

Chapter 5

Area 5: Re-Align Resources (People, Time, Talent, Energy, and Money) to Support the Instructional Focus.

FOUNDATIONS

Area 5: Re-align resources (people, time, talent, energy, and money)
to support the Instructional Focus.

- Take a look at all you have . . . start the hard conversation . . . allow all items on the table.

- Make decisions around what students need, not what makes adults comfortable.

- Direct your resources to your area of Instructional Focus.

- Tie realignment of resources to improvement in teaching and learning.

Insufficient resources are often blamed as the main reason we don't see more success in our schools. As school and district leaders ourselves, we often wished we had a little more money, another teacher or two, or more office support. As we have worked across North America and with the worldwide Department of Defense school system, however, we have come to believe the amount of resources is not as important as how we use the resources we have.

There are surely "bottom lines" for people, time, and money that can't be reduced without catastrophic results. However, we have seen high performing schools where the level of support is $4,000 per student per year and very dysfunctional schools where the level of support is $19,000 per student per year. Karen Hawley-Miles has done some wonderful thinking in this area, and we base much of our work on her ideas.

There are four key ideas to consider when aligning resources.

• **Take a look at all you have . . . start the hard conversation . . . allow all items on the table.**

When schools begin to align resources around the Instructional Focus, there is often a tendency to see current conditions as fixed. However, most money in any school's budget is committed to personnel. This is as it should be, but sometimes schools have accumulated personnel who no longer provide the most efficient service needed to assure all students master the Instructional Focus. Often these are very nice people who are a part of the congenial culture of the school. It is difficult to talk about eliminating their positions in order to provide more professional development, acquire critical resources, or change personnel for someone more suited and better trained to meet student needs. It can also be difficult to cut special programs or pet projects that are good in themselves but divert time, energy, or other resources from the most important instructional program.

It is crucial that schools begin resource allocation from ground zero. Consider every position, every program, every minute, and every staff member as they relate to the Instructional Focus. This will enable the faculty to identify which resources strongly support learning. Those resources that are less than a powerful contributor to student learning should be redistributed or eliminated.

- **Make decisions around what students need, not what makes adults comfortable.**

Change is hard. There is just no way around that. Anyone who thinks you can dramatically improve the performance of a school without making adults uncomfortable is dreaming. There is no blame involved here. It is often the case that the adults are working hard and doing the best they know how to do.

The problem is often more organizational than personal; schools are not organized to address the complex needs of today's student populations. When making tough decisions about realignment of resources, a staff must be willing to consciously put the needs of the students first. This does not mean that we advocate hours and hours of time outside the workday, or that staff need to donate lots of their own personal time for professional development or tutoring students. It can all be done during a reasonable workday, as we have seen in many situations, but the necessary changes in established patterns will require staff to accept a period of uncomfortable adjustment for the sake of the students.

- **Direct your resources to your area of Instructional Focus.**

Society asks schools to do many good and important things. As this list grows over the years, however, it becomes no longer possible to accomplish all of those good things with the resources provided.

Most schools will need to STOP doing some good and important things in order to fully succeed at the most important thing which they have identified as their Instructional Focus. Do we really need to take up ten to fifteen minutes of prime instructional time each morning for intercom announcements? Could we take school pictures, offer bike-safety programs, and hold PTA candy sales during non-instructional time?

All resources—time, people, and money—need to be aligned to support the focus. In many cases, we find that other important things are picked up by community agencies or happen before or after school. Some programs end up being dropped altogether, perhaps an indication that they were not as important as someone thought.

- **Tie realignment of resources to improvement in teaching and learning.**

The primary function of a school is not to serve as a community employment service; sports training program; or gang-, drug-, and pregnancy-prevention center. The primary function of a school is to develop literate, responsible citizens. Yet many schools and school systems spend enormous amounts of their limited resources on activities that do not support that primary function.

Systems need to reexamine practices and policies around resource allocation to ensure they are doing everything possible to support high-quality teaching through ongoing targeted professional development, frequent teacher collaboration and planning, and consistent monitoring of implementation. Any people, money, or time allocated to support anything other than promoting high-quality teaching and learning should be very closely scrutinized and dropped or revised unless an exceptionally strong defense can be made for the allocation.

GETTING STARTED

- **Stop doing some things to free up resources for your focus.**

Once school and district leaders identify their Instructional Focus, it becomes easier to decide how to use their resources—time, people, and money. Often, leaders decide to stop activities that do not support that focus to free up resources and support activities that do. For example, some schools reworked the job descriptions of non-classroom personnel (aides, clerical, and some specialists) to increase their impact on the focus area as support for instruction in the focus.

Others stopped doing pull-out programs (they just don't work in most situations) and instead provided support for special needs students in regular classrooms. Not only did this assure high-quality teaching, but it greatly reduced the need for remediation. Still other schools realigned the use of specialists by assigning them back into regular classrooms to reduce class size at certain grade levels or in certain subject areas.

• **Use research to help you reallocate resources to support your focus.**

Schools and school systems have approached resource reallocation in many different ways. However, after studying the research, we have developed twelve Guiding Principles that may help you redirect your resources in ways that enable to meet your instructional goals.

There are several things to remember as you use these principles. First, they are designed to embrace many possible solutions and strategies; not to suggest there is one solution for every school. Second, they vary in importance depending on each school's specific strategy and progress in implementing that strategy. Thus, schools will benefit from reexamining these principles in relationship to their practices and goals every year.

Finally, they must be accompanied by instructional change to raise student achievement. We know many schools reduce student group size with no effect on achievement because they fail to address the teaching and learning taking place in those smaller classrooms. We have seen how creating longer blocks of instructional time makes little difference if teachers do not receive additional professional development, where needed, in using that time effectively.

Below are twelve findings that research shows tend to guide high-performing schools, help them meet their instructional goals, and improve student achievement. See "Rethinking the Use of Teaching Resources: Lessons from High Performing Schools" by Karen Hawley Miles and Linda Darling Hammond for more details.

Resource Allocation: 12 Research Findings

High performing schools allocate *time* to:

1. Incorporate common planning time for teachers into the everyday school life so they can look at student work together, reflect on teaching practices, plan instruction, and share best practices.

2. Maximize time, including longer blocks of uninterrupted time each student spends on the Instructional Focus.

In high performing schools, *teaching staff and students are grouped* to:

3. Use smaller student group sizes and reduced teacher loads and better meet student needs in the Instructional Focus. (For example, minimize specialized and "pull-out" programs for specific groups of students and teachers.)

4. Vary student group sizes based on educational needs, not on staffing formula, and allow for variation over the course of a day.

5. Promote more personal relationships between students and teachers.

6. Redirect resources from redemption to prevention.

High performing schools *organize and hire teachers and other adults in ways that:*

7. Deploy a larger percentage of teachers to work in the academic focus area.

8. Shift resources and responsibilities from support and administration to instruction.

9. Use significant resources for professional development that supports the school's Instructional Focus.

10. Make full use of policies to hire new staff that fit the school's needs.

High performing schools *use programs and funds from private and external sources* to ensure that:

11. All additional school programs and funds—including funds from special programs and external and private sources—support the Instructional Focus and educational plan.

12. Technology is integrated as a tool to support the Instructional Focus.

DISTRICT SUPPORT

In this case, knowledge is power. Districts that are most successful in supporting schools provide them with accurate information about the resources available to them and give them wide latitude in reallocating those resources within a structured framework for improvement in teaching and learning.

Many superintendents refer to this as "bounded autonomy." Schools are given significant control of their own resources **as long as those resources are all utilized around the improvement of teaching and learning.**

STORIES FROM THE FIELD:
Business Services Leads the Way

When the Yakima, Washington School District began to rethink its work with the goal of providing better service to its customers—schools, the Business Services Department realized they needed to better understand the needs of schools. To this end, the assistant superintendent of Business Services decided if his department was to become an integral part of the district's improvement effort, all of the supervisors and managers in his department should attend professional development training with the school principals. His reasoning was they would know what the schools were hoping to achieve, understand the challenges they faced, and be better skilled at understanding how they could support the schools' allocation of resources.

The members of the Business Services department took advantage of this professional development to further the work of the department. When schools had time to plan as school teams, the Business Services department met as a group with a consultant to discuss what they had learned and how they could support the initiative. They talked about what they could do to streamline their services. These meetings represented a significant realignment of their time and personnel resources.

They learned a lot about the schools' attitudes toward central services and what schools perceived were roadblocks from the district. They were surprised sometimes by what they learned. Requests they made of the schools, which they had deemed reasonable, apparently were not so reasonable. They learned the schools felt pressured by some requests and did not think central services understood schools very well.

Their findings led them to challenge themselves to streamline their services; provide helpful, targeted, and wanted support to schools; and support the district's literacy initiative.

Going back to school. *The Business Services department made a point of doing more of their business in schools. First, they addressed the complaint of central services not understanding schools, and reallocated time to enable the administrative staff to visit schools, attend principal and teacher workshops, and observe first hand how the work of their departments impacted the daily life of schools. This face time was well received by school leaders, built relationships between school and district leaders, and strengthened communications between the staffs.*

They restructured the agenda of the department's monthly planning meetings to focus on how to streamline their service, reduce the paperwork, and condense the demands they made of schools. They tried a variety of ideas; some worked and others did not, but all efforts were appreciated and discussed with their "clients"—the schools.

Taking action to support the focus. *The Transportation Division of Business Services researched how they could support literacy through their work. They met with the district's bus drivers, shared the district's literacy plan with them, and worked together to think about how they could reallocate resources and support the initiative.*

They decided each bus would have a box of books, arranged by grade level, located next to the driver's seat. Children would be invited to take a book to read as they entered the bus, if they did not have one of their own. Books were donated or provided by the Teaching and Learning department. The bus drivers all wore buttons that said, "We Love Reading." They even redesigned the bus safety program to center around characters from popular children's stories.

The plan was a huge success. It caught the attention of the media and was featured in the local newspaper. This was a simple plan that proved to be highly successful and certainly made a statement about transportation's support for schools as they worked to improve their students' reading skills.

Customer Service Survey. *As they deepened their understanding of the vital and difficult work the schools do on a daily basis, the central services staff decided they should develop a customer satisfaction survey.*

They had already been in contact with other districts to ask them how they handled service to schools and a survey was suggested.

It was a bold step—the first customer satisfaction survey from a central services department in the district. The members of the department expressed excitement and nervousness about the survey—what would it tell them? They determined they should conduct the surveys themselves, not wanting to impose more work on the principals. They requested a ten minute slot at a staff meeting, explained the purpose of the survey and asked the teachers and staff to give them honest answers. Their questions related to efficiency, effectiveness, and customer orientation. They were brave enough to break down their Business Services department by area so that they would get a read on each specific area, (i.e., transportation, accounting, technology, food services, and maintenance.)

They could not wait to get the results and analyze them. They were generally delighted with the positive results and it also provided them with areas for growth. They developed graphs and charts and wrote a report, which went to the Board of Trustees and was shared with all principals. As a follow-up they decided to set up small focus groups in schools to get more information where they did not score as well as they wished. The focus-group meetings went exceptionally well, and valuable practical suggestions were made to improve the various services offered by the Business Services department. Their suggestions have been considered, and they are being implemented wherever possible.

The survey will be an annual event, which will be copied by other central services departments. The school principals and staff were positive about the sincere effort made by this department to gather honest information about their service. In this case the Business Services department provided an excellent example of how to rethink its use of resources.

TOOL FOR LEADERS

Zero-Based Budgeting: One Possible Scenario

Zero-Based Budgeting is a process for aligning resources to support an organization's priorities. It is especially helpful when there are not enough resources to fully support all of the good things the organization would like to do. Zero-Based Budgeting involves the following six steps:

1. Identify the priority (Instructional Focus)
2. Set SMARTe goals for improvement
3. Identify improvement strategies necessary to meet goals
4. Compute cost of improvement strategies
5. Identify resources to support improvement strategies
6. Allocate remaining resources where needed

In schools, Zero-Based Budgeting begins by reviewing data to identify the Instructional Focus. The school then sets SMARTe goals for dramatic improvement in student learning in that Instructional Focus. The third step is to decide what it would take to meet those challenging goals (this might include things such as professional development, more instructional materials, content specialists or coaches, expanded learning time, etcetera.)

Each of these improvement strategies needs to have a price tag connected to it (some, such as creating an expanded instructional block of 120 minutes for the Instructional Focus, or changing the reading teacher's job description to that of coach, doesn't cost anything.) The total cost of these items becomes the priority for the budget.

The goal is to fund these strategies first and then distribute any other resources to other areas. It is often the case that some programs or some non-teaching support positions will need to be converted to funds to fully support the priority area.

Use the following activity to review and discuss a scenario that introduces Zero-Based Budgeting as an approach to resource allocation that supports an Instructional Focus.

Steps for Activity:

1. The facilitator explains that the participants will have an opportunity to have an overview of Zero-Based Budgeting, a process that helps align resources to improve teaching and learning in the Instructional Focus.
2. Briefly introduce the ideas above by teaching the six steps. Provide participants time to read the scenario below and discuss in small groups.
3. Allow time for clarifying questions about the six steps or the scenario.
4. Have participants return to small groups to discuss the following:

   • How does this process compare to the way we usually allocate our resources?
   • How might this process help us better align our resources in support of our focus?
   • What challenges might this process create for us?

5. Allow time for open sharing or questions across the groups.
6. Give participants time to plan how they will approach resource allocation alignment this year.

Scenario

The student performance data at Lincoln Street School showed that only 15 percent of the students were reading or writing at grade level according to state standards. The entire school community worked together to identify literacy as their Instructional Focus, and set the goal that all students would be performing at grade level within three years.

The staff met and identified several instructional practices that they believed would help accomplish this goal. They felt that the most important improvement had to be in regular classroom teaching, and that they would need a lot of professional development to become expert at utilizing the new strategies in their classrooms. They compiled a detailed professional development plan that they felt would lead to the expertise needed, including weekly after school training sessions (in instructional practices, assessment, and data review and use), peer coaching of implementation of the training, joining national reading and writing organizations, setting up book study groups, videotaping lessons for personal review, weekly collaborative planning sessions, coaching support from a literacy specialist, and released time for observing each other.

A committee then investigated the cost of each of these interventions and brought the total to the Instructional Leadership Team (ILT). The ILT and principal found the resources to support the professional development plan by converting several classroom aide positions, and using most of the supply budget as well (local businesses were then contacted by the principal to donate the necessary supplies for the year.) This same process was repeated the following year, and the school met their goal a year early.

Chapter 6

Area 6: Engage All Families and the Community In Supporting the Instructional Focus

FOUNDATIONS

> **Area 6: Engage all families and the community in supporting the Instructional Focus.**
>
> • Create two-way communication with all families and treat them as valued clients.
>
> • Focus communication on ideas that will help all students show growth in the area of the Instructional Focus regardless of individual student differences.
>
> • Help the whole school community understand what good work looks like in the area of the focus.
>
> • Develop a common understanding of how home and school work together in ways that promote the academic achievement of all groups of students.

The Rand Corporation has done a wonderful job of researching the connection between families and schools with regard to student learning. Their findings consistently support the belief that when families are engaged in and supportive of the school, students learn more. Unfortunately, life in our complex twenty-first century seems to make it increasingly difficult for each student to have that kind of support. We have seen many places where the definition of "family" has been expanded to include any adult who provides care and supervision for a student, and still struggle to have each student's "family" be aware of and engaged in the student's learning at school.

When many of us were in school, it was common that almost 75 percent of households had someone attending a local public school. A notice sent home with students or an event that engaged students would impact the majority of the local community. Now that number is less than 25 percent in many places, providing schools with limited opportunities to interact with a majority of the community. Even though this presents a great challenge to schools, there is much that can be done to generate the support students need if we are to meet the goal of ALL students achieving at standard.

Focus on Results has centered our work on four key concepts that can help schools develop effective parent and community involvement.

- **Create two-way communication with all families and treat them as valued clients.**

It is essential that parents and other community members are viewed and view themselves as equal partners in the education process of our students. Many schools state this belief but do not seem to act on it. Few schools have places and practices that help parents and others feel comfortable and valued when they come to the school. Many school-home communication plans are designed as one-way models, rarely collecting ideas from home about what is working and what might make things better.

One school we worked with implemented a strategy for two-way communication that revolved around Response Journals. Each student was given a nice, hardcover journal on the first day of school, and wrote the name of their primary caretaker on the front cover. At least once each week—usually Mondays—the teacher would staple a short form into the journal with check marks showing how well the student had been doing the week before, listing any missing assignments, and giving the homework for the week ahead. In addition, the teacher would write a short note to the caretaker. The opposite page was reserved for the caretaker to write a response or ask questions and to sign indicating that they had seen the teacher's note. Each classroom kept track of how many students returned the journal on Tuesday—with the caretaker's signature.

All classes achieving the standard of 90 percent or more for the month received an award certificate to post in their room and a bonus time of twenty minutes of free reading in place of any other subject that day. They saw a dramatic increase in family engagement as a result of this two-way approach to home-school communication.

- **Focus communication on ideas that will help all students show growth in the area of the Instructional Focus regardless of individual student differences.**

Since it is so difficult for families to make time for engagement with the local school, it is essential that any communication or activity designed for their participation is one that directly impacts student learning in the Instructional Focus. Many schools use families and community volunteers primarily as fundraisers. While this may be a necessary evil in some settings, creative schools have found ways to blend fundraising with learning; having Read-a-thons instead of jog-a-thons, selling books instead of candy, or engaging community members for fundraising instead of parents and students.

Likewise, any printed material sent home should be about the Instructional Focus, including data about how well the school is doing in that area, examples of student work or assignments in that area, specific suggestions for things to do at home to reinforce learning in that area, etcetera. All communication should reflect appropriate language and cultural considerations as well.

- **Help the whole school community understand what good work looks like in the area of the focus.**

We have never met a parent or child caretaker who wanted their child to fail at school; there may be some, but in thirty years we've never met one. Most families want their children to do well and wish they could help more.

The best way to help families help their child is to provide clear examples of what the student needs to learn, along with examples of how the student is now doing. It is often not a good idea to have parents actually teaching their child at home. However, when families know what their child is supposed to be learning, they can see the importance of learning. They can see that their child's current level of performance in that area is below standard, and will often do whatever we ask of them in terms of support and collaboration. For example, some schools using a rubric for scoring student writing will have parents score an occasional paper and then compare their student's work to an exemplar of good grade-level writing. This often leads families to encourage and motivate the children in ways absent before.

- **Develop a common understanding of how home and school work together in ways that promote the academic achievement of all groups of students.**

Schools often offer Parenting Classes as a general panacea for poor parent involvement; this seldom works unless requested by the parents and connected directly to supporting student learning. What we have seen work better is when schools decide amongst themselves exactly what they need from families and devise ongoing communication plans to inform and equip parents with the necessary information and skills to be able to deliver what the school has identified.

For example, if a school decides it is essential for student success that students extend the learning day by doing homework, the school needs to both inform families of their role in supervising the students during homework time, having a quiet place for homework, limiting other family activity during homework, etcetera. The schools that do this most effectively also provide families with a number to call if the student is having difficulty with the homework as well as a place to bring students for quiet workspace if there is none at home.

GETTING STARTED

As principals, we believed family involvement to be essential for students to achieve at their highest level and found ways to assure not only that every family was involved, but that the students understood the expectations for their family as well. To do this we had to redefine the term "parent involvement" and began with meeting the families where they were. One of us visited the families—all five hundred-plus of them—at home to help them see the importance of their involvement. Another of our schools had "mandatory" family involvement contracts that gave parents and caretakers options for involvement before school, during school, at home or at school, after school, evenings, and during weekends. They were also expected to assure each student did at least an hour of homework each evening, and to be sure their child was "ready to learn" each day—physically, emotionally, and psychologically.

We also invited family adults to our professional development activities, so they would know what we were learning to do and why, and we used monthly evening meetings as interactive learning opportunities for students and their families—not as opportunities for them to come and listen to us talk.

One of our schools had one Family Fun Night each month focused on a different curriculum area. The teacher experts for each area would plan interactive centers that embedded content into their literacy focus. The experts would share these centers at a faculty meeting along with all materials necessary and each class would participate at the centers on the afternoon of the Family Fun Night. After a half hour of dessert potluck, parents and students would go to their classrooms and students would help their parents with the activities at the centers— explaining what they were learning. This proved to be an invaluable strategy for building support with families as we implemented some new and potentially confusing instructional practices (such as using manipulatives in math, activity-based science, and balanced literacy approaches in reading.)

Another school we worked with saw its parent involvement and support soar after they implemented a program of meeting with parents on Saturday mornings once per quarter for "teacher listening" sessions. The teachers would use a half-day professional development block and go home early. They would exchange this time for coming in to school on a Saturday morning, when parents were more available.

At the "teacher listening" sessions, the school provided breakfast for families (donated by a local Burger King), activities for children (supervised by a local recreation department), and met with parents in their children's classrooms. Each teacher asked two questions: "What is working well for your child in this classroom?" and "What do you think would help your child learn more in this classroom?" Teachers were not to answer or defend parent's concerns or suggestions, just to listen closely and chart their suggestions and concerns. The parents were told the teachers would meet together to share their charts and wherever possible create ways to implement changes to improve the learning environment. They went from having ten or twelve adults attend their "parent meetings" to having more than 80 percent attend the Saturday morning family sessions.

DISTRICT SUPPORT

As in other areas we have discussed, districts can support this work by organizing resources centrally to help all schools develop these family partnerships. For districts that serve families of many languages, the district should offer translation services to ensure each school has the ability to communicate with its diverse families.

In large districts where students attend schools out of their neighborhood, many districts arrange bus service on family nights to help parents come to the schools for evening and weekend events. In addition, many districts arrange partnerships with local agencies, churches, Boys and Girls Clubs, and community centers to allow evening and weekend events to be held in the families' community so parents do not need to travel out of the area to attend school organized functions.

STORIES FROM THE FIELD:
Increasing Family Involvement

Schools and districts that build deep connections with families and community ask those families to partner with them on their improvement agenda. The district leaders in Edmonton Public Schools wanted to make sure their families were more closely tied into the district focus on improving results for all students.

Much of the district's drive grew out of their urgency around improving the high school completion rate. Internal district studies had shown students' early elementary literacy levels were directly related to their likelihood of completing high school. Many of the district's educators understood the connection and knew this was information families should know as well.

To help spread this message, the district created a series of informational newsletters, bulletins, and media stories highlighting these issues. They didn't stop there. More importantly, they created tools for every school to use and share with their families to help this information reach every parent. They also provided training for school leadership teams and for family and community leaders to get this message out that early literacy is critical for high school success.

Here is a sample taken from the actual training material the district developed for schools to use with parents and community members to help to make sure the community understood the link between early literacy and high school completion, and enlist specific support from the community. The training materials help to lay out the fact and rational for the district initiative. With the combined strengths of school personnel and community support and encouragement, the district has been able to dramatically improve student performance and graduation rates in the high schools.

Edmonton Public Schools:
Community Training Material
Superb Results from All Students: Our Common Focus

In our community, we have been working hard to support all students to achieve superb results in literacy and numeracy. We have made much progress. However, over the last two years as a school district, we have realized an even greater emphasis on teaching and learning is required of us to ensure that ALL students are producing superb student learning results, ALL students are completing high school, and ALL students are *prepared* to attend school beyond high school if they choose.

In today's session we will share together:

1. An aspect of the information that has helped us arrive at our districtwide focus on teaching and learning.
2. The *correlation* between superb results in reading and the likelihood of completing high school.

3. A snapshot of results from a typical school that has been focused on teaching and learning.
4. Time to think and plan together about our own school community.

What do we know?

1. *About the need to complete high school?*

Benefits: Increased Levels of Education Lead to Increased Employment

In Canada, in 2002:
- 21 percent of those Canadians who obtain less than grade 9 are employed.
- 72.6-77.1 percent of Canadians with some post-secondary training (trades, university) are employed.

Benefits: Increased Levels of Education Lead to Increased Levels of Income

In Canada, in 1996:
- The average earnings of Canadians with less than grade 9 or grade 9 to 13 earn approximately $18,000-$19,000.
- This increases for Canadians with post-secondary education (trades, university) to a range of $25,000-$42,000.

2. *About the number and percentage of students who COMPLETED high school over time?*

Our district investigated how well we were doing with supporting ALL students to complete high school and found

- The results for Edmonton Public Schools show that five years after students began Grade 10 in 1995-96, 63 percent of students had completed high school.

- The results for Alberta at this same time show that 72 percent of students had completed high school.

We also know as a district that the numbers are not good enough. We know we need to prepare all students to be able to complete high school. *We also know this is a challenge that can only be met when all schools, preschool, elementary, and junior, and senior high work together with families and the community around a common focus on teaching and learning.* That is why over the past two years our district has developed a relentless focus on supporting teaching and learning. This is why schools have developed a solid focus on instruction, implemented sound instructional practices and held themselves accountable for measurable growth in student learning for ALL students.

To further this end, our school system researched the connection between student success in reading and their likelihood of completing high school.

3. *What do we know about the connection between reading and high school completion?*

Our research found that

- In general, the lower a student's grade level of achievement in reading upon entering high school, the less likely the student is to complete high school. This relationship is remarkably stable. The relationship holds true for both cohorts that were tracked for five years. The relationship also holds true for the 1998-99 cohort that was tracked for three years. In addition, within each cohort the relationship holds true regardless of gender.

- The charts below summarize the key findings from our research. Note on the first chart the dramatic drop in the likelihood of high school completion for students who were only ONE YEAR behind in reading.

Students who read at Grade 8 Level in Grade 9	43.0 % completed high school after five years
Students who read at Grade 9 Level in Grade 9	69.8 % completed high school after five years

The pattern repeats itself when looking at elementary schools. Note on the next chart the dramatic drop in the likelihood of high school completion for students who were only ONE YEAR behind in reading

Student who read at Grade 5 level in Grade 6	37.3 % completed high school after three years
Students who read at Grade 6 level in Grade 6	59.0 % completed high school after three years

The trends are quite similar. It is information such as this that has helped us as a district and a school develop a tighter and more consistent focus on the improvement of teaching and learning.

What are we doing about this?

Information like this is one of the chief reasons schools at all levels have been working with great passion over the last two years to increase their focus and support for the improvement of teaching and learning.

Each school in Edmonton Public has

1. Developed an area of Instructional Focus to improve student learning
2. Found ways for teachers to work together and pool their professional knowledge

3. Selected and implemented evidence-based teaching practices
4. Provided targeted opportunities for staff to develop their skills in these teaching practices
5. Allocated their resources around what's best for student learning
6. Involved families in the work of supporting teaching and learning
7. Held themselves accountable for the improvement of student learning by setting measurable goals for improvement

We realize that it is prekindergarten—grade 12 efforts of teachers, schools, and families working together to support ALL students to complete high school.

We are already seeing some clear results in student learning. Schools are identifying through local measures sustained improvement in students' reading and writing.

High schools are tracking and have noted, in many cases, improved rates of completion in core academic courses leading to high school completion. Each high school has set a target of increasing its completion rate this year.

Here we see the data from one school, who, with a relentless focus on improving teaching and learning was successful over a three-year period.

To read this chart, simply follow the bar graph three years in a row. The graph shows the progress of the SAME group of students over a three-year period. The graph shows that after two to three years of focused work, 100 percent of students were reading at grade level in nearly all cases.

Although this success does not guarantee that these students will complete high school, data shows that they are far MORE likely to complete.

HLAT Reading Results: Comparisons from 1999-2002.

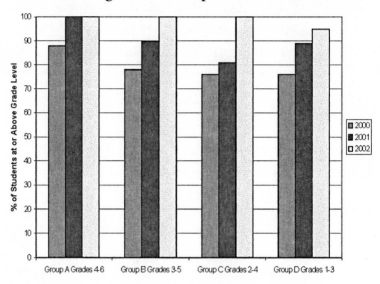

NOTES:

The 2002 results are official. The comparisons show the same group of students over the past three years. The percentages include one student who also moved to the school in this year.

Grade 1 in 2000 at Grade 3 level in 2002—one student not at Grade Level
Grade 1 in 2001 at Grade 1 level in 2001 and
Grade 2 level in 2002—one student not at Grade Level

What are we doing? What could we do next?

Now let's take some time to discuss how this larger information impacts what we are doing in our own school community. It's clear that, at our school, we have been working on many of these issues as well. This is an opportunity to remind ourselves about the work we have already accomplished and steps we have yet to take.

Use the following handout in small groups to discuss the key questions and use the handout to take notes. At the end, each group will be asked to share out some key ideas and possible next steps. The school's Instructional Leadership Team will take these notes and summarize next steps for our school.

What Are We Doing?	What Could We Do Next?
To share with our community the district data on high-school completion and reading?	
To improve our students' ability to read at grade level?	
To share our school-level data with our community?	

The success of the training is that it helped to involve families, in a substantive level, with the real information about the need for school improvement. The district was free to share its challenges, express what the plans were, and ask families to help. It proved to be a high quality way to involve families and the community in the genuine work of improving teaching and learning for all students.

TOOL FOR LEADERS

There is a large and ever-increasing amount of research that shows that close school—family partnerships lead to powerful student learning. Yet it can seem overwhelming for a school with a history of low cooperation to move toward a culture of collaboration and trust with its families and community. Joyce Epstein has formed a national network of schools that are wrestling with these same issues and finding many useful ways to address them.

This tool enables a school to review the *Six Keys of Successful Partnerships* that Epstein's schools have discovered and select just one or two likely to yield results quickly and build a foundation for future collaboration. It is important to remember that both school staff and parents need to review the Six Keys and recognize the unique contribution of each before deciding which key to target first.

Assessing our Progress on the Keys to Successful School—Family—Community Partnerships

In small mixed groups of family members, community members, and school staff, fill in the box for "What We Are Doing Now" for each of the Six Keys. Identify which ONE key you think could be an area for the partnership to address that would yield improvement quickly and build a foundation for future collaboration. Share your ideas with the other small groups and discuss options until agreement is reached. For that ONE Key, generate suggestions to put into the "Possible Next Steps" box and return those to the leadership committee.

	What We're Doing Now	Possible Next Steps
PARENTING: Assist families with parenting and child-rearing skills, understanding child and adolescent development, and setting home conditions that support children as students at each age and grade level. Assist schools in understanding families.		
COMMUNICATING: Communicate with families about school programs and student progress through effective school-to-home and home-to-school communications.		
VOLUNTEERING: Improve recruitment, training, work, and schedules to involve families as volunteers and audiences at the school or in other locations to support students and school programs.		
LEARNING AT HOME: Involve families with their children in learning activities at home, including homework and other curriculum-related activities and decisions.		
DECISION MAKING: Include families as participants in school decisions, governance, and advocacy through PTA/PTO, school councils, committees, and other parent organizations.		
COLLABORATING WITH THE COMMUNITY: Coordinate resources and services for families, students, and the school with businesses, agencies, and other groups, and provide services to the community.		

From School, Family, and Community Partnerships, by J. L. Epstein et al., ā 1997 Corwin Press. Inc.

Chapter 7

Area 7: Create an Internal Accountability System Growing Out of Student Learning Goals

FOUNDATIONS

Area 7: Create an internal accountability system growing out of student learning goals.

- Set schoolwide goals that are *s*pecific, *m*easurable, *a*ttainable and challenging, *r*elevant, *t*ime-bound, and touch *e*very student (SMARTe Goals).

- Check all students every six to eight weeks in your area of Instructional Focus using a school-based measure.

- Use the data to drive continuous adjustment to daily instruction, paying particular attention to achievement gaps among student groups.

- Using the language of results for all students, promote and celebrate student-learning gains shamelessly.

The collection and use of data is the seventh and final area of focus because, like the first, it weaves its way through each of the other areas. It is the only true indicator that all of the other work is worth doing. It drives and refines both classroom instruction and school leadership. It provides the initial sense of urgency needed to mobilize for improvement and provides ongoing motivation to fuel the continuing improvement efforts.

It is often difficult for schools to implement Area 7 because of the way student performance data has been used in the past. Many claim that "data is just a tool." Unfortunately, the tool most often associated with student performance data is a hammer, and it is used to beat schools and educators over the head for poor performance levels. As a result, schools tend to shy away from using student data and have even generated a national movement to discredit testing and assessment as unreliable, invalid, or unnecessary.

Our experience suggests real improvement comes only when schools are willing to face the facts—however brutal they may be—and frequently monitor and discuss the impact of their improvement efforts.

- **Set schoolwide goals that are *s*pecific, *m*easurable, *a*ttainable and challenging, *r*elevant, *t*ime-bound, and touch *e*very student (SMARTe Goals).**

Mike Schmoker has provided us with definitive research on setting goals. It is virtually impossible to argue with his findings and suggestions, yet we visit school after school that have no clear goals for improving student performance. This seems to be partially due to a fear of failing to meet the goals and partially due to a lack in understanding of how to set good goals.

As a result, we have developed our SMARTe Goals process. This process leads schools through a review of their current data on student performance using a "Red Flag" approach. It then helps them to set a few goals for where they want to be, goals that are

- *Specific*—describing exactly what students will be able to do.

- *Measurable*—without being too intrusive to the instructional time. A common and admirable goal is students become lifelong learners. While we certainly hope all students do, this is not a good goal for a school to set; to measure it, you would have to wait for the student to die and then interview friends and family to see if the deceased had learned anything new recently. A facetious example, certainly, but one that is indicative of the "safe" unmeasurable goals schools too often set.
- *Attainable yet challenging*—a staff has to believe the goal is something that could be reached yet has also to recognize that it will not be reached if they keep doing the same things; it can only be reached through significant effort and change in practice. Business as usual won't get us there.
- *Relevant*—since we are only setting two or three goals, each one needs to be something very important and connected to success in real life, not just in school.
- *Time-bound*—addressing all the issues of time—how often, how long, by when, etcetera, and
- Touch *every* student. This is the only way we will be able to narrow the achievement gaps between racial, ethnic, and primary-language groups and regular and special education.

These goals then drive all other decisions about internal accountability, as well as teacher collaboration, evidence-based practices, professional development, resource allocations, and parent involvement.

- **Check all students every six to eight weeks in your area of Instructional Focus using a school-based measure.**

When we start school in August or September, it is essential to have clear goals for where we want to be in June. However, too many schools that have goals seem to simply cross their fingers, close their eyes, and hope that they will get there doing whatever it is they have planned for the instructional program. Even the spacecraft that actually made it to Mars was off course most of the time. Despite all those fancy computers on board and back home, NASA cannot predict everything that will happen. These guys really are rocket scientists, but they still know not everything will work out as their brilliant minds planned. The on-board and on-land computers talk to each other continuously, making repeated adjustments to the trajectory.

We need to do the same thing in schools. We need to monitor student progress toward the SMARTe Goals at least every six to eight weeks, especially for any students who have previously shown to be below standard.

- **Use the data to drive continuous adjustment to daily instruction paying particular attention to achievement gaps among student groups.**

Phil Schlechty is fond of saying something like, "No matter how often you weigh the pig, don't expect to see a sharp increase unless you change how you're feeding it," and he's right on the money. Collecting data every six to eight weeks or more frequently won't, by itself, help students learn more. Only when teachers are given time and structures to organize, analyze, collaboratively discuss, and use the data to adjust their instructional practices will we see the kind of improvement needed. The previous section on teacher collaboration teams (Area 2) provides more details on how this is best accomplished.

- **Using the language of results for all students, promote and celebrate student-learning gains shamelessly.**

By language of results, we mean being very specific about how many students have improved, by how much, and in what specific skill. It often helps to be specific about which students as well. There are subtle taboos in some schools about comparing the progress of some students or some classrooms, even as a celebration. We somehow feel everyone working hard equates with everyone being as effective as others. This is often not the case and only when we begin to be comfortable discussing the fact that "twice as many of the students in room 8 are performing at grade level as in the other two second grades" will we ever be able to identify differences and apply effective strategies more uniformly.

Short-term wins can provide motivation for staff, students, and parents to continue with the hard work of change. This is the best possible use of data, and we should take every opportunity to celebrate the fruits of all our hard work!

GETTING STARTED

Building an internal accountability system that drives action.

There are six actions that should take place when building an internal accountability system that drives changes to teacher practice and student performance as follows:

1. Set an Internal measure by which to monitor student performance every six to eight weeks.
2. Start a frank and honest assessment of current reality based on data.
3. Set rigorous SMARTe goals for the improvement of student learning.
4. Turn the data numbers into real students that cannot be ignored.
5. Create plans for those students and hold people accountable for following through.
6. Continue to monitor student progress and adjust practices to meet SMARTe goals.

1. Set an Internal measure by which to monitor student performance every six to eight weeks.

The first key concept to consider when building an Internal Accountability System is beginning with the end result in mind. *"The end"* you keep in mind is the SMARTe student learning goals/targets you have set both for *external* (state, provincial, and national) measures and *internal* (local school-based) measures.

If you do not have a local internal (school-based) measure yet, you cannot set a SMARTe target for it.

Decide on at least one way to measure internally how your students are growing in your area of Instructional Focus to set the *internal* SMARTe Goal. As soon as possible, work with your Instructional Leadership Team (ILT), staff, and central office to develop or select an initial measure or instrument you can use with all students to take a baseline in your area of Instructional Focus. This could be a locally developed writing, problem-solving, or open-response prompt to which all students respond and are then scored by the staff. It could be a diagnostic reading assessment that as a school you are comfortable with or even a simple reading-comprehension assessment you give to all students. The key is to get a baseline you can use to help set a SMARTe target and monitor throughout the year.

We have used a variety of assessments at our schools—Running Record, Scholastic Reading Inventory, Developmental Reading Assessment, schoolwide writing prompts utilizing site-based rubrics, end-of-unit tests from texts, teacher-made tests, criterion-referenced tests, and standardized norm-referenced tests. There are lots of assessment options available— the important thing is to find one that measures student performance in your area of focus that you can give to students every six to eight weeks so you can track progress throughout the year.

At our schools, we stressed the need to monitor each student in our area of focus and to collect data about their progress so teams of teachers and the principal could sit together and discuss how to get even more progress—especially from any student who continued to be below grade level. We were then able to celebrate our success shamelessly and publicize it as often as possible.

Be careful not to get caught into the trap of overanalyzing the merit of each possible local measure. We have seen school teams and district leadership spend months of committee meetings and debates looking for the "right" measure(s). Yet as the committees met and agonized, students and teachers worked away without an organized and systemic way to monitor that kids were reading, writing, solving problems, and thinking critically any better than they had the month before.

It is simply important to select with your ILT a measure or measures to help you *get started* as quickly as possible, creating this local system to monitor and adjust instruction based on student-learning needs. The first measure you select and begin to use might not be perfect. Only through the experience of the professionals in the building who use it will you know. The experience of using it, talking about it, and sharing student results from it will inform you staff's conversation. The key is to *get started* even if the first measure is an "off the shelf" product. If it will help get the staff thinking about the need to monitor student learning on a regular basis, it is worth trying.

STORIES FROM THE FIELD
Communicating Your Local Indicators of Student Achievement to the Public

It is important to communicate your local indicators of student achievement to the public so they are valued as much as standardized test scores. One school always had PTA volunteer positions for public relations. Their job was to get at least one positive report about our school into the local newspaper each week. The position was handled as it would be in business. They took reporters to lunch to explain the focus, goals, and progress. They wrote drafts of stories for them always with some reference to the gains they were making, including charts, graphs, illustrations from excel, and reporting everything in numbers— percentages of students at level or percent of improvement in the number of students at grade level since September, etcetera. They worked with political figures to get support for a special weekly supplement on the local schools in the newspaper. They volunteered for radio talk shows and local cable broadcasts. All of this built expectations the school was academically focused and continuously improving.

As standardized scores followed local performance measures in improvement, these volunteers produced high quality tri-fold flyers that were distributed to businesses and service organizations in the community showing charts and graphs of improvement, and soon, realtors were telling a very different story about the school. A variety of state and federal organizations began to contact the school regarding award and recognition proposals. The volunteers treated these seriously and found funding to engage the whole faculty in receiving these awards.

As this story reveals, we firmly believe it starts with identifying some specific local measures in the focus area to administer, monitor, collect, display, publicize, and celebrate as a way to build momentum and expectations of achieving our challenging goals of high achievement for all of our students.

2.   Start a frank and honest assessment of current reality based on data.

Start in the most basic of places. Ask people to sit down together and look at what the data said about their current reality. Do not attempt to overdramatize nor marginalize the picture the data painted. Through careful facilitation, help people identify "just the facts" presented by the data. Give people simple and easy-to-read data and have them discover the answers to these questions such as

— What number and percentage of students scored at what levels?
— How does that information compare to the school or district data?

Make sure you have participants write down their answers. This basic paper-and-pencil exercise is a key element in making these sessions useful. Instead of a talking head up front, analyzing the data for the staff, and then spitting out the findings, this process allows the group to work together to arrive at answers to their own questions. The act of actually writing their findings down cements the information in a concrete way folks can remember. Do not, however, stop your work here. Use this grounding in current reality to help set the stage for what is next.

3. Set rigorous SMARTe goals for the improvement of student learning.

Use some simple key questions to help the faculty think about where they want to be by the end of the year. Ask questions such as

- What is *our* goal for our students?
- What percentage of students do we want to be at proficient or above by June?
- What percentage of students do we want to be at proficient or above by June as a *grade level?*
- What percentage of students do we want to be at proficient or above by June *in my classroom?*

Use these key questions to spark discussion and debate. They raise issues of expectations and beliefs in student and teacher efficacy. The leader or facilitator should make sure these discussions lead to goals the faculty believes in and can stand by with pride.

When weak draft goals are offered, such as "3 percent of our students will improve this year," the leaders can parrot them back to their staff and ask them if that was good enough. More than one principal helped their staff frame the issue as families would see it. Imagine telling your families at school night this year we expected "3 percent of our students to improve." What about the other 97 percent? We had all hoped our student was in that 3 percent group. Generally the school that develops the strongest goals followed a formula Focus on Results has adapted for educational use. They used the acronym SMARTe to "litmus test" their goals.

One school's example of a solid goal is as follows:

> One hundred percent of our students will show improvement in their writing ability as demonstrated by the districtwide writing prompt administered three times a year for grades K-12. No less than 75 percent of students will show growth to the *next* performance level. The remaining 25 percent will show growth *within* their performance level.

4.   Turn the data numbers into real students that cannot be ignored.

Take the conversation to the next important step by asking staff to move beyond setting the goal. Ask folks to take the numbers and turn them into real students whose faces they see nearly every day. Work to create a personal connection with these students to help people realize they are not simply meeting a goal. They are working to transform students' lives. Ask questions such as

- What are the names of the students who performed best on the most recent measure?
- What instructional practices are being used with those students?
- What are the names of the students who performed in the lowest categories on the most recent measure?
- What instructional practices are being used with those students?
- Do any patterns appear concerning those students? (e.g., gender, race, primary language)

Do not simply ask the questions and let them fall into an unfocused intellectual conversation that does not follow to action. Instead, provide staff with some clear instructions and a concrete protocol to structure this conversation. Here is one school's example of such a protocol.

Step 1   Each teacher brings his/her own local assessment data to the team meeting. Be sure everyone in the group is familiar with the data and can make sense of the information provided.

Step 2   Each teacher works independently to identify how many students are scoring at each level in each category, using a graphic organizer.

Step 3   Each teacher works independently to identify the names of students scoring at each level in each category, using a graphic organizer.

Step 4   The team reviews each teacher's data chart to discuss the following questions:

1. On which assessments are students performing best?
2. What instructional practices are being used in the areas assessed?
3. On which assessments are the greatest number of students farthest from the goal?
4. What are the names of those students?
5. What patterns appear concerning those students (e.g., gender, race, primary language, etcetera)?
6. What instructional strategies are currently being used in the areas assessed?
7. What changes in instruction might improve student learning for students farthest from the goal?
8. What additional support or interventions do these students need?
9. What additional resources or professional development might be needed to implement adjusted instructional practice?

Use this protocol or others like it to help leaders define, organize, and support teachers as they work through the data. These facilitated meetings help teachers use their time on activities productive for them and fosters increased collaboration and dialog as well as improving the quality of support developed for students.

5. **Create plans for those students and hold people accountable for following through.**

Even the best of team meetings, with the greatest protocol, the most insightful and collaborative conversation, and produces seemingly the most brilliant plans, often comes to naught if folks aren't supported and held accountable for *follow through*. Who is committing to do what? by when? and when will we meet again to check on progress? Build these details into accountability plans. Schedule follow up meetings. Visit classrooms to support teachers and check on students' progress. Ask essential questions such as

- What changes in instruction could improve student learning for students scoring in the lowest categories?
- What additional support or interventions do these students need? Okay, if this is true then . . .
- What instructional strategies do we agree to try with students scoring in the lowest levels?
- What support/interventions will we provide for students scoring in the lowest levels?
- On what date will we meet again to discuss what we are learning from trying these teaching strategies and creating these interventions and supports? (No more than two weeks.)
- What additional resources or professional development might be needed to implement adjusted instructional practice?

Time and time again, it is the use of these six simple questions that have helped leaders make their *use of data actually drive action*. Some schools and school systems are more effective than others in using their current student-learning data to drive action around the improvement of teaching and learning. Clearly one of the bedrock beliefs in these schools and systems is the commitment to dramatically improve the academic achievement of each and every student regardless of race, gender, ethnicity, language, or socioeconomic factors. Excuses for low academic performance based on any of these factors are unacceptable.

With that as a stated moral authority, school leaders may engage their school community in *questions* around the data and then hold people accountable for action. The schools should ensure these questions are asked in multiple settings, with multiple audiences, so that the entire school community may become more **knowledgeable**, more **responsible**, and more **accountable** for the improvement of student learning.

Reject the impulse to blame increased accountability as the chief nemesis. Don't allow the ugly spiral of victimization to take hold in the corners of your school or district office. Instead, use these new challenges to push your organization forward into concrete actions that you can take to improve learning for every student.

6. **Continue to monitor student progress and adjust practices to meet SMARTe goals.**

The key here is in revisiting the data often. Students who are below level need to be assessed at least every six to eight weeks in order to determine if the planned interventions are actually being successful. If there is progress, the strategies should be continued. If there is no progress, the strategies must be reexamined. They may wind up being continued for another cycle, or perhaps modified or intensified, or they may be dropped all together. All good strategies do not work with all students, and it is important to identify which strategies work best with which students in order to build on those strategies over time. It is essential that we not keep doing the same thing over and over even when we see it clearly isn't working, but to make properly informed decisions, we must have current data throughout the year.

TOOL FOR LEADERS

Accountability Academy

The purpose of this tool is to help district and school staff to develop a deep understanding of what a rigorous Internal Accountability System looks like. Faculty and staff may then apply this knowledge to the development and evaluation of their own Internal Accountability System.

To use this tool, first introduce and have participants read the following excerpt on **Accountability Academy.** This reading describes what a rigorous Internal Accountability System looks like when fully implemented into the life of a school.

As participants read, ask them to use the **Accountability Academy Reflection Guide** (printed at the end of the excerpt) as a note-taking device. In small groups, have the participants share, generate, and record their insights, questions, or ideas on their reflection guide. Finally, hold a large group debrief around the key concepts developed through the investigation of the Accountability Academy.

Discussing Accountability Academy is a good place to start the conversation on Internal Accountability Systems because each participant in the discussion will likely see things they can connect with from their own experience, yet few will have been a part of such a comprehensive approach.

It is important to stress to those discussing this example that this is not considered the template all schools must emulate—it is just a composite of many different options one school might utilize.

Accountability Academy:
An Example of a School with a Balanced Assessment System for Monitoring Student Progress

Welcome to your tour of Accountability Academy. The first part of the tour will be guided, as we take you through each of the key centers at our school that impact our Internal Accountability System. After the initial tour, you will have the option of returning to any particular location that interests you to do further investigation regarding that aspect of our plan.

The Entrance: As you enter Accountability Academy, the first thing most people notice is our welcome banner. The banner states,

> Welcome to Accountability Academy. It is our goal that ALL activities that occur at our school are designed to improve student learning. Our emphasis is on results, and we have developed a Balanced Assessment System for Monitoring Student Progress that guides all of our work here. The Score Card displayed in the main hallway will give you a good idea of how well we are performing on our SMARTe GOALS in our focus academic areas. In addition, copies of our School Accountability Report Card are available in the Office. If you have any questions about student performance or the Internal Accountability System itself, please ask anyone you see; as all staff, students, and parents are involved and informed in all aspects of our results emphasis. Please sign our Visitor's Book at the Greeters' Table and enjoy your visit.

We feel we have a strong responsibility to keep our community informed about the effects of the work we are doing at our school and want everyone to know as soon as they enter our building that we are focused on student learning. The banner has been an effective way of notifying visitors and reminding us and our students of the purpose of coming to school each day.

Assessment Conference Room: The next stop on our tour is the Assessment Conference Room. This room is actually used for many different purposes each day, but some of the most important work that goes on here is Data Review by the Instructional Leadership Team (ILT). At the beginning of our plan, all existing data on student achievement was collected and carefully reviewed by the ILT. Using a prioritizing process (Red Flag Data), the ILT identified several specific areas of low student performance and wrote SMARTe Goals to address those. The SMARTe Goals targeted improvement in our schoolwide focus of literacy on standardized tests (Stanford 9, Iowa, Aprenda, MCAS) and student performance in reading and writing. Our entire school community—staff, students, business, and community partners—was involved in finalizing and approving these standardized test and student performance goals.

Assessment Research Corner: Across the hall from the Assessment Conference Room is our Library/Information Center. Most of the books for students have been coded by reading level and moved into classrooms where they will get more use. As a result, computers connected to the Internet for research by both students and faculty now occupy most of our Assessment Research Corner. This corner contains a great number of books and articles our staff has collected from classes, journals, and the Web. After SMARTe Goals were set, study groups of teachers, administrators, and parents were formed to examine what the research said about appropriate assessments and practices that would help us monitor student progress toward our goals. Some of the assessment ideas we chose were drawn from the training we receive with our literacy model and some we chose from other sources to create a balanced program. One of our ongoing study groups continues to monitor and update our Assessment Research Corner, and every article here has been read by at least three members of our staff who decide if it should be discarded, retained in our center, or copied for all staff and distributed.

Assessment Resource Center: As we move to the rear exit of the library, we come to a small room that we call our Assessment

Resource Center. While many of the assessment packages and tests that we explored are available on the Web, we also keep hard copies in this room. Each of the assessments we use regularly for reading level and writing level are kept here in quantity for ready use by teachers as needed. At our school, we have identified assessments and created packets for English, Spanish, and Vietnamese readers. All students are assessed at least every other month in reading and writing in their primary language and in English with the emphasis on developing dual fluency. One of our teachers receives a stipend for maintaining materials in this center.

Classroom in Action: Walking down the hallway of our West Wing, you can notice several evidences of classroom-assessment practice. Since this is during our three-hour uninterrupted literacy block, we won't actually go into rooms, but much can be noticed through brief glances through the open doors and by observing the clusters of students working in the hallway.

Outside room 8, for example, notice how the students are working in pairs, editing each other's writing. The rubric for this assignment is on the chart posted just outside the door. These students are working well, and make it look easy, but it is important for you to know that they have had training in the writing process and peer editing for two years. Also, they practice this with many writing assignments, doing another draft before it is turned in for teacher evaluation leading to a final draft. Student work posted outside room 10 clearly shows the elements of our writing assessment system. These papers are from our monthly schoolwide prompt. The prompt itself was taken from the questions released by our standardized test provider. Notice that for each student, their prewriting notes are displayed next to their initial draft and their revised draft. The chart in the center shows the writing level of each of the students on this assignment. This way, students are able to see progress in their own work and compare that to the exemplars that are posted as well.

If you peek quietly into room 11, you can see a teacher using the Diagnostic Reading Assessment with a student. This assessment combines Running Record with comprehension questions and is given individually to about two students each day while the other students are working at centers. This approach allows us to update the reading level of each student every six to eight weeks.

Celebration Center: As we walk down the hallway past the cafeteria, we can see the photographs and footnotes posted here that commemorate all of the different celebrations classrooms have had this year when they have shown improvement toward our SMARTe goals. Some of the celebrations have included ice cream or pizza, and some have involved sharing student work with families. Most of the celebrations involve students, but some of the pictures show awards and ceremonies for teachers and staff as well. The Celebration Center is located here so students waiting to enter the cafeteria are reminded of the rewards of their hard work and of our schoolwide emphasis on results.

Assessment Conference Room—Looking at Student Work: Our tour schedule suggests we return to the Assessment Conference Room at this time. What you will see there now is a group of teachers and support staff collaborating in a process called Looking at Student Work. Teachers look at student work all of the time in their own classrooms, of course, but this process allows them to compare the student work to specific standards, exemplars, and standardized assessment objectives in a collaborative setting.

The examination of the student work is conducted in a structured process that leads to substantive conversation about the real issues of teaching and learning and is an invaluable tool in helping to identify patterns in student performance—allowing teachers to adjust their instructional strategies to address specific student needs. Having other teachers and support personnel involved in the study of the students' work provides multiple perspectives and serves as a resource to increase a teacher's repertoire of alternative instructional strategies. Each of our teachers is a part of a Teacher Collaboration Team that meets for ninety minutes twice each month for this Looking at Student Work process and meets every other week for forty-five minutes of collaborative planning.

Schoolwide Scorecard Display: As we leave the LASW group, I want to be sure to point out our Schoolwide Scorecard Display here in the main hallway. We have placed the display here because it is the most visible spot in our building and we want everyone— staff, students, parents, and visitors—to be continuously reminded of our focus and the results of all of our efforts. As you can see, the Scorecard displays percentages of students reading on grade level by classroom and grade; percentages of students writing on grade level by classroom and grade; percentages of students performing at each of the levels on MCAS, Stanford 9, Aprenda, and the Iowa TBS by classroom, grade, and schoolwide; and the average daily attendance of students by classroom, grade level, and schoolwide.

Reading percentages are collected and posted every other month demonstrating increase throughout the year; writing percentages are posted each month, as they are drawn from that month's schoolwide writing prompt, allowing comparison month by month; standardized test scores are posted for the three most recent years; and attendance data are posted monthly.

Head Learner's Office: Another very important place for us to visit is just down the hall and to the right. This is our principal's office, who has placed a sign "Head Learner" over her office door. The sign serves as a constant reminder to all of us that we are all engaged in continuous improvement, constantly learning how to do our job better. The heart of the Balanced Assessment System is to provide us with data to help steer that continuous improvement process.

Our principal spends a lot of time reviewing student data to identify trends or patterns and developing materials to share this information regularly with the staff and families. Sometimes the principal meets here with individual teachers to work out plans for specialized professional development of instructional improvement. Sometimes the office is empty or used by others while the Head Learner is out walking through classrooms or observing a particular lesson as part of our instructional leadership plan.

Everyone in our entire school community knows student learning is the number one priority of our principal and that she is continually trying to learn how to help us all back in the Assessment Conference Room. Last month's LASW sessions identified a weakness in most grades with students writing clear explanations of how they solved problems in math. We will be having one of our ongoing workshops this afternoon with our literacy-coordinator as part of our thirty-six hours of professional development that will focus on modeling strategies to address this weakness, and our principal wants to go over the data with our school change coach before the session.

ACCOUNTABILITY ACADEMY REFLECTION GUIDE

Complete this graphic in small groups—be prepared to share responses.

Key Issues in Each Paragraph	How Do We Address Each at Our School?	Questions or Concerns about Each	What Else Do We Do?

Here are some other ideas schools and districts should consider as they begin this work.

ELEMENTS OF AN EFFECTIVE INTERIM MEASURE

Elements	Details
Curriculum Relationship	• Task reflects outcomes in standards/programs of study. • Task targets the instructional focus. • Task is specific to the subject context.
Task Design	• Identifies outcomes being measured. • Provides clear instructions for the student. • Focuses on measurable student performance. • Aligns with classroom instruction. • Takes prior student knowledge into consideration. • Makes provision for the range of learners.
Scoring Considerations	• Criteria are derived from outcomes. • Various levels of performance are defined for each. • Language clearly distinguishes between one scoring category and the next. • Rubric/scoring guide is applicable to a number of contexts so students and teachers begin to internalize. • Over time rubrics/scoring guides may require updating.

What are some questions we can ask ourselves as we think about finding/ selecting/developing these local school measures?

What **measures** are we already using but perhaps not schoolwide?

- Review measures currently in use
- Discuss strengths and limitations of each

With what **frequency** are we using these measures?

- Discuss how frequently the tools are currently being used
- Discuss strengths and limitations of current use

What **feedback loop** do we have in place to share the data we collect?

- Discuss that the feedback loop is how data will be collected, displayed, and used to adjust instruction

- Discuss how data will be collected after each tool is used
  — Who will collect?
  — Who will organize for display?
  — Will this be done by computer or by hand?
  — By when must data be submitted each time a tool is used?

When are we ready to implement our local measure and what are things we should think about?

Materials

- What materials will be needed for each measure?
- Who is responsible for ordering materials?
- Where will they be kept?
- Who is responsible for keeping them organized/replenished?
- How will teachers obtain materials needed?

Training

- What training will be needed for teachers to use each measure?
- Who is responsible for organizing the training needed?
- How will the expenses for the training be covered?
- Will substitutes be needed to allow teachers to practice?

Schedule Changes

- Will schedule changes be needed to allow teachers to administer the measure to all students at the beginning of the year?
- Will schedule changes be necessary to allow teacher teams time to review data and adjust instruction?
- Will schedule changes be necessary to train all teachers in each of the tools?
- Are there any other changes to the schedule that might be necessary?

Reporting System

- What data will be reported externally as well as internally?
- How will this data be displayed to show improvement over time?
- What audiences will receive this data?
- How frequently will progress be reported?
- Will students take a more active role in reporting their learning?

Things to STOP

- What will you **stop** so you can begin this?
- Can you simplify report cards if you use this system?
- Can you stop using other curriculum assessments?
- Can this be combined with your Looking at Student Work process?
- Can this simplify your data review process for school planning?
- Can this be used for grant applications and school evaluation?
- What other things could you stop?

Chapter 8

Leadership That Focuses on Results

Some schools have outstanding results, with all or almost all students meeting or surpassing rigorous standards. Many schools do not have such strong results. Some systems have a large percentage of high-achieving schools, while other districts have few, if any, high-achieving schools. For a long time, this has been explained in terms of socio-economic status (SES) and primary language, with race and ethnicity considered—though often unmentioned—contributing factors. Recently, however, more and more examples have been surfacing where urban, multi-ethnic schools with students whose primary language is not English and whose families qualify as low SES are somehow seeing the same outstanding results as the mono-cultural, mono-lingual, and affluent suburban schools. As we have worked with some of these schools and studied others—the single striking consistency is leadership.

In our experience, schools that show dramatic improvement in student learning are schools whose leaders are transformational leaders, instructional leaders, reflective leaders, and intentional leaders. We have not found there to be one "perfect" leadership style, but rather that the effective leaders operate with a combination of each of the four types of leadership. This chapter will share our perspectives on what each of these types of leadership looks like in an improving school; how they work together to create the culture needed for rapid growth; and how the types of leadership impact the different levels of leadership for teachers, principals, central service administrators, and superintendents.

The following quotes reflect aspects of the type of leadership we have seen in continuously improving schools:

"In times of change, the learner will thrive, while the learned will find themselves beautifully equipped to deal with a world that no longer exists."—Eric Toefler

"It is not so important how many followers one has, as it is how many leaders one creates."—Ralph Nader

"Some lead by power, some by deceit, but with the true leader, when the task is finished the people will say, 'We did it ourselves.'"—Lao Tzu

"In leadership, the main thing is to keep the main thing the main thing."—Jim Clarke

Transformational Leadership

Steadily improving schools have leaders who are passionate about their work and about their students. They have a deep sense of moral commitment that drives their day-to-day decision making. One superintendent with whom we work frequently reminds those on his staff, "Our work is nothing less than transforming the lives of fifty thousand students." In order to fully serve each of their students, these leaders are willing to reexamine and transform any structures, practices, policies or roles. They understand minor adjustments here or there are not going to be enough and have the courage to embrace wide-scale change. They utilize their positions and their personal power to engage others in support of the necessary transformation, and they help stabilize the transformation during the rough spots by reminding others of the justice of the ultimate purpose.

These leaders are not always "charismatic" or even overly dramatic in their work. They are just clearly committed to do whatever it takes to meet the goal that drives their internal passion. They recognize it will take a lot of work and a lot of time to get there, but they are willing to invest in the long-term, deep-level commitment the transformation will require.

Instructional Leadership

Steadily improving schools also have leaders who realize the key to improved student learning is improved instruction, and they focus on this relentlessly. They recognize that the secret is the magic that happens between the teacher and the children in the classroom, but they also know magic happens more frequently in some classrooms than in others. Helping each teacher achieve a high standard of excellence is the core of the work for instructional leaders.

The greatest part of the work that Focus on Results does with schools and school systems is in helping each member of the community be focused on this goal of excellence in instruction and equipping them with the proper tools and strategies to be able to do this efficiently. The Seven Areas of Focus are all about providing a framework that will empower each member of the school and district community, and direct support necessary to achieve excellence in every classroom. This does not mean, however, that the only way to be an instructional leader is by following the Seven Areas and using Focus on Results tools. We have gone to many schools, and a few districts where staff at all levels were struggling with these issues and had achieved significant success through their collective wisdom. Even in those situations, additional improvements were seen when the focus became clearer, overt, and systemic to all leaders.

Instructional leaders demonstrate their interest in a number of ways. First and foremost, they are, or they immediately begin working toward becoming excellent instructors themselves. As Roland Barth says, "You can't lead where you won't go." To be a true instructional leader, you must have a deep knowledge about what good work looks like in teaching.

In a number of subject areas, understanding good work means having quite a bit of content knowledge as well as knowing appropriate instructional practices. This need for deep-content knowledge is one of the reasons it is so essential there be a number of instructional leaders on any staff who are ready and able to provide the support and accountability necessary to guarantee every classroom provides truly excellent learning opportunities for each student. The need to develop true expertise in instructional strategies as well as deep understanding of background and content is also one of the reasons we so strongly encourage schools to focus on a single instructional area as they begin their transformation.

Instructional leaders also recognize the need for continuous learning. They do not see themselves as the expert who has all the answers but rather as one who will be constantly developing their skills and increasing their knowledge base. The primary method of growth that we have observed is through collaboration. Instructional leaders create multiple opportunities to talk with others about their work. Sometimes they read and discuss articles; sometimes they arrange for others to observe them in action and discuss what they have seen; sometimes they use a protocol to examine student work and talk together to make connections to their own teaching; and sometimes they go to other settings to observe promising practices other schools and districts have developed. Whatever processes are used, the emphasis is on continuous improvement. This is partially what makes education a true profession and separates it from the trades. There is always more to learn, always possibilities for improvement. It is like the little boy in the desert who asked his father, "Are we there yet, Papa?" The father could only reply, "My dear son, please remember we are nomads—we are never there." Instructional leaders recognize this yet find ways to help others celebrate increments of progress made.

A third way we have seen instructional leaders demonstrate their interest is by putting their time where their mouth is and being in classrooms frequently. For principals, we encourage a goal of 50 percent of each day in classrooms; for superintendents, at least 20 percent of each week; and the same for teacher leaders to be in other teachers' classrooms or with other teachers in their classroom. Time spent in the classrooms seems to be most useful when it is focused time—looking for specific instructional practices that everyone knows about, training in, and is working to master. This is not about catching mistakes and not really about evaluation. Very, very few teachers need to be dismissed, but many teachers need to be helped to improve.

The behaviors of instructional leaders when in classrooms that lead to the most improvement include providing demonstration lessons—with follow-up discussion about what worked and why; team teaching with the regular classroom teacher and discussing the process afterward; observing a lesson and giving coaching afterward; or taking over the class so the regular teacher can visit another room or meet with other teachers to further instructional excellence. In addition to these strategies, we have seen great value in regularly visiting each classroom for five to seven minutes, often called a walk-through, to get an overall view of what is happening in instruction throughout the school. This information is critical to making good decisions about professional development activities and resource allocation.

The final way instructional leaders demonstrate their interest is in how they allocate resources—time, people, and money. We discussed this earlier in chapter 3, but it bears repeating. Schools simply do not have enough resources to do everything society asks them to do. Where we have seen schools engaged in continuous improvement, we have seen instructional leaders who targeted all resources toward excellence in instruction—even at the cost of some good traditional programs or activities; even at the cost of eliminating staff positions that were helpful, but not as important as excellence in instruction or even at the cost of upsetting some teachers who have been working very hard but need to change their methods in order to reach all students.

Reflective Leadership

Most schools we visit could be characterized as being guided primarily by the *tyranny of the urgent*. That is to say that what is most important right now is what gets the attention of its leaders. There are so many things going on at any given time and so many mini-crises always in flux in the lives of the students and the staff that it is very difficult not to be in a perpetually reactive mode. One of us who was a school leader for more than twenty years often remarks he had a plan for what to do every single day of those twenty-plus years yet not once in all that time did he actually get to follow that plan. Substitutes don't arrive and classes must be distributed or staff reassigned; a child-abuse situation comes up just before school starts and requires the attention of the entire student-support team for the next three to four hours; an adult shows up who wants to pick up a child yet the custodial parent has made no arrangements with the school and cannot be contacted to verify permission, etcetera. It is very easy for school and district leaders to become caught up in the daily drama of these important issues and be continually trapped in reaction rather than systemic, pro-active improvement.

At schools and districts where student learning is steadily improving over time, however, we consistently find evidence that the leaders there have found ways to build in time for reflection—time alone or in small groups to consider what the current practices are, what impact those practices are having on student learning, and what else might be done to improve the impact and increase the learning. The reflection time always includes data to inform the thinking and always leads to a plan for specific actions toward improvement of the data. In some cases, these are weekly meetings with the superintendent and cabinet that take priority over anything other than true emergencies; in some cases, it is a weekly hour without interruption the principal spends going over data and information from student work or assessments and classroom visits, or in some cases, it is a grade-level or cluster team of teachers who meet to look over data on student work or performance and create plans for adjusting instruction accordingly. It is always difficult to carve this time out of busy schedules, but it seems to be critical to do so.

Lorraine Monroe, a highly successful principal in several schools in New York City, tells how she scheduled a weekly conference with a very important person from the community and let everyone on her staff know this person was so important she could not be interrupted. She met with this person for an hour each week at each of the schools where she was principal during her career. There was, of course, no such person; she just knew how important it was to regularly schedule extended time to reflect on her leadership and the results it was producing. She has frequently credited this practice with contributing significantly to the improvement at those schools.

From our experience as successful educational leaders and from our ongoing work with other successful educational leaders over the past ten years, we believe creating time to be a reflective leader is one of the essential elements in improving student learning. In our work with districts, one of the pieces we always include is some form of peer coaching. An effective peer coaching model would include a minimum of a one or two-hour visit each month with someone who is currently or has been recently in the same position to talk over what is being done, what impact it is having on student learning, and what else might be done to improve the impact and increase the learning. In some cases, we are the coaches, but in a large district, we train district personnel in our Results-Based Coaching model and help them create a schedule to initiate regular coaching sessions. This is one way to help leaders recognize the value of time spent in structured reflection, and it often results in having those leaders identify additional time and strategies for weekly reflection.

Intentional Leadership

In our work, we often have the privilege of visiting highly successful schools where all students are learning at high levels and ask them to tell us their story—how it got to be this way. Yet in all of our one hundred-plus combined years of work as educators, we have never once visited a highly successful school and been told that "It just happened; we all came to school one morning and all of a sudden everything was great! All the teachers were teaching in powerful ways and all the students were learning at dramatically improved rates." On the contrary, we have found that every highly successful school has a very interesting story to tell about the change process they went through, and it was usually about how hard it was and how long it took. Every single time, leadership is one of the key ingredients. There was a vision, there was a sense of urgency, there was a specific plan developed, and there was guidance to implement and adjust that plan. This is what we mean by intentional leadership.

Intentional leaders do everything for a purpose. They know where they are going. It is not accidental. They do not just stir up passion and commitment and then cross their fingers and hope for the best. They do not just put out good ideas through articles and models and inspiring professional development and hope for the best. They do not just study the current conditions, reflect on ways to improve, and hope they somehow happen. They do all of these things, but then they do the hard work of guiding the district or school community to assure what needs to be done really happens, and it happens in every classroom, in every school, for every child.

Intentional leaders also do not wait to be told what to do. They are constantly looking for the next step in their continuous-improvement process—just the right set of materials, just the right new staff member, just the right model or trainer, just the right place to go visit. Even though they are already very busy, they make the commitment to stir up the waters when necessary, rather than sit back and consider their current situation to be good enough. At the same time, intentional leaders do not just accept and implement whatever comes down from above; whether above is the nation, the state, the superintendent, the district, or the principal. Instead, intentional leaders sift the new directive through the lens of their plan and purpose. They accept what moves the plan forward—

usually with modification. If a directive arrives "from above" that conflicts with their plan and purpose, they resist or quietly ignore it. It may be impossible to follow every rule, implement every directive, include every new politically-motivated program at a school and still see all students learning at high levels.

Intentional leaders do only what they know will work to further their well-studied plan of action. It is our experience that results are the best defense in these situations, though not always enough. While it can be important to pick one's battles, it is also important to realize intentional leaders must have sufficient moral commitment to choose what is best for their students rather than what is always politically expedient. In the words of one educational leader we know, "To be successful in education—leading schools where all students achieve at high levels—you must always know what you'd like your next job to be and be prepared to go do it if the need arises."

Steadily improving schools have leaders who operate in all four of these types of leadership. They feel and generate passion and commitment to the task of transforming the lives of the children served; they monitor instruction on a regular basis to assure effective practice in every classroom at every school for every student; they gather a variety of data and create time to reflect on what's working and what needs to be improved; and they are very intentional about their leadership by having a clear plan that everyone knows and by doing the hard work of following through to see that all aspects of the plan are fully implemented.

A Note on Collaboration in Leadership

If ever there was a time when the leadership of one single person was enough to produce powerful results in a school or district, that time is past. Schools and school systems are so complex as organizations, so complicated as legal agencies, and so challenging as multi-layered cultures, it now requires many different leaders to be able to meet the standard of high achievement for all students. It further requires all of those leaders work in concert toward the same goals and via the same plan of action. Some of the leadership is positional, but some of the most influential leadership is informal and comes from a sense of shared beliefs and commitment to common goals. Only through close collaboration can these leaders hope to see those goals accomplished.

In our work in schools and school systems, we have seen collaboration demonstrated in a variety of ways. At a visit to one school, the principal informed us her staff was very collaborative—they always agreed with ideas the principal put forth. After a very short time at the school, it became apparent the staff was not collaborative at all; they were not really even involved in leadership. They were happy to defer any decisions to the principal and then went about doing what they had always done. There was only one leader, but that leader had very few followers. This is not collaboration.

In another setting, a superintendent complained his principals were not collaborative—they were constantly challenging his good ideas for improvement. Further investigation showed the principals agreed the ideas were good, just coming too fast and without reasonable plans for implementation. The superintendent and the principals shared the same beliefs and the same commitment to common goals. However, as long as the superintendent saw collaboration as instant agreement, little progress could be made. This is not collaboration.

When collaboration works, it looks more like this: a culture exists where disagreement is valued, as long as it occurs within a set of articulated shared beliefs, common goals, and norms for discussion. Leaders at all levels are involved in deciding how to implement improvements and how to measure progress toward implementation. Expectations are very clear, so there are no "gotcha!" surprises and a culture of trust underlies the collaboration. All staff is empowered to take leadership in accomplishing the goals, and everyone is supported in developing the capacity necessary to fully implement the improvements. This type of collaboration must be embraced by leaders at all levels for a system to operate at peak efficiency.

Positions of Leadership

Superintendent:

In all systems where we have worked, the superintendent is a key gatekeeper. He or she permits or rejects the entrance of improvements. Sometimes it is done in subtle ways, simply allowing change to happen without acting to stop it or withholding support and allowing it to die off. In districts where we have seen the most rapid improvements in student learning, the superintendent actively embraced the changes, speaking publicly about the plan, and providing encouragement during the rough spots. It is our belief that the active support of the superintendent is essential for a system to see significant gains in student learning.

One of us recently conducted a study of superintendents who have seen significant gains and has identified several key leadership factors that contributed to those gains. Each of these superintendents focused their energies, time, and resources around promoting, supporting, and developing the instructional leadership of their principals. These superintendents used eleven different, though related, strategies to promote the role of instructional leader for their principals. These strategies fall into three categories.

Superintendent Actions for Promoting Instructional Leadership:

Setting the Focus on Student Learning. Including actions such as the following:

- Establish new district vision focused on student learning needs
- Establish minimal district goals for student learning and performance
- Engage principals in values/beliefs reflection about high expectations for all students

---

Setting Clear Expectations. Including actions such as the following:

- Establish the primacy of the instructional leadership role of the principal—both verbally and in writing
- Define instructional leadership for principals
- Establish standards for principals tied to evaluation and merit pay

Holding Principals Accountable for Acting as Instructional Leaders. Including actions such as the following:

- Implementing superintendent and assistant superintendent site visits and walk-throughs focused on instructional practice with written feedback
- Aligning the supervision and evaluation process with the Instructional Focus, including review of student performance data

Individual schools can certainly make progress without the full engagement of the superintendent, but those gains seldom survive long in a system that is not responsive or with a superintendent that is not supportive.

Principals:

Much has been written about the importance of the principal to student achievement. We have each experienced that to be true both personally and in our work with other schools. This is truly a key position. In our work with large systems we have found that there is not just one type of principal successful at implementing transformational change leading to dramatic improvement in student learning. Given a clear framework for action and given appropriate tools and training, we have seen hundreds of principals from different types of backgrounds and with a wide range of personality and leadership styles be successful.

The key here seems to be a willingness to do the hard work of collaboratively designing and monitoring the implementation of an instructional improvement plan built around intensive professional development in evidence-based instructional practices. Combined with this is a willingness to deal with upset staff members who will be impacted by the need to change practice or by the required changes in resource allocation. When growth doesn't happen at a school we are working with, it is most often due to a principal who wants to be liked more than they want improved student learning or due to a principal who just doesn't want to do the hard work of assuring full implementation of a quality instructional improvement plan.

Of course, there are probably a lot of principals who just don't know what to do, or who don't feel they would be allowed to do what they know—by their district, or their teachers' union, or whomever. There is no easy cure for this. As discussed earlier, true educational leaders must be instructional leaders and principals must be continually studying what works in order to know what to do. Having an external group provide training and coaching support is very helpful but others have found the necessary information and support from local sources as well. Chapter 3 of this book provides an excellent framework with which to begin. For those who are dealing with concerns about permission or resistance, we can only say courage is one of the essential aspects of leadership for the principal. It is simply not okay to hold back until improvement will be easy; the principal is often the last hope the students have for a high quality education and a transformed future.

Teachers:

In improving schools the key unit of change is the classroom. We can no longer settle for islands of excellence; the only way to achieve the goal of being a truly effective school—where all students are achieving at high levels—is to have every single classroom providing excellent instruction for every student, every day. During our work with schools, we have seen this requires four things:

1) Intensive professional development to a deep level of expertise for all staff in specific, schoolwide, evidence-based instructional practices.

2) Structured collaboration opportunities for teams of teachers to look at student work together, share assignments with an eye toward improving the quality of assignments given, and helping expand our range of effective instructional strategies. At a school we are only at our best when all know what each of us knows.

3) An open culture of practice where teachers, the principal, and others frequently observe each other teaching, frequently walk through each other's classrooms and have multiple opportunities to discuss what they have seen in collaborative conversations focused on continuous incremental improvement.

4) Structured engagement of teachers in planning and decision making through the creation and development of an Instructional Leadership Team. This team, comprised of the principal and five to ten teachers from a range of grade levels and content areas, only collaborates on issues and all decisions directly impacting teaching and learning.

Only when each of these is firmly in place do we begin to see the consistency of high quality practice in each classroom leading to improved learning for all students.

The leadership challenge inherent in establishing this type of open culture occurs when teacher leaders are the ones to propose it, encourage it, and assure its full implementation with other teachers. A top down edict from a superintendent or principal is simply ineffective by itself. Teacher leaders at each site must see the value of this culture and be courageous enough to support it with their peers. This is often more difficult than it sounds. We have seen numerous situations where the improvements stalled at this level. There is often a pervasive culture in schools that all teachers with more than two or three years experience are the same, or at least equal in their ability and knowledge. It is felt deeply that one teacher should never be in a position to evaluate the work of another teacher.

This is often connected to an underlying, unspoken belief that the results one teacher gets with his or her students is due more to the students themselves than to the work of that teacher. In our experience, nothing could be further from the truth. The work of each teacher is crucial and the work of each teacher on a staff often looks very different from the work of other teachers on that staff. Teacher leaders should not be asked to evaluate other teachers, but they must be willing to evaluate the work of other teachers in a culture where everyone—including each leader—makes their work public in order to consistently improve that work. Our students deserve nothing less.

No school ever became a highly successful school—where all students were learning at high levels—by accident. In every case, the improvements were a result of powerful, collaborative leadership; leadership that was transformational, instructional, reflective, and intentional. And in each case the leadership was evident at multiple levels within the school or school system. Without this kind of leadership, our high standard of success for each child simply cannot be reached.

TOOL FOR LEADERS

In the area of leadership development, we have seldom come into low performing settings and found teachers who were highly engaged in leadership focused on instructional issues. By contrast, we have seldom seen high performing settings where teachers were not directly engaged in instructional leadership decisions. For this reason, the tool we have selected to share in this leadership chapter concerns the development of the school Instructional Leadership Team (ILT).

THE INSTRUCTIONAL LEADERSHIP TEAM

The Instructional Leadership Team's primary role is to help lead the school's effort at supporting the improvement of teaching and learning. The ILT meets regularly, makes decisions about the school's instructional program, and leads and monitors the implementation of a sound Instructional Focus.

What the ILT IS:

- Focused on student achievement
- Centered on teaching and learning
- Fully committed
- A model of a learning community
- Knowledgeable about how students learn
- Unique to each school
- A place where divergent ideas are heard and leadership is shared

What the ILT IS NOT:

- Additional responsibilities for an existing committee
- Composed of only those who happen to be available
- An elite group
- The Governance Council (ILT members may also serve on the Governance Council)
- Responsible for the day-to-day business of the school (although they may make recommendations)
- Dominated by one person or group

The ILT MEMBERS ARE:

- School leaders (formal and informal, catalysts, and motivators)
- Reflective of multiple perspectives and diverse opinions
- Representative of the school community
- Committed to leading the long term improvement process to better their school and provide their students with the best
- Willing to tackle tough issues and take risks together
- Supportive of other team members, encouraging each others' participation, expression, and ideas

The ILT DOES:

- Consider school activities and decisions to ensure that they are consistent with the Instructional Focus
- Meet regularly and frequently (at least twice a month)
- Hold themselves mutually accountable for their responsibilities and for improving student performance
- Learn (through formal training, reading, self-study, reflection, and conversation) about the improvement process, and what works to make good schools better
- Maintain clear objectives and a clear agenda for each meeting
- Guide the school's whole school improvement plan
- Develop a process to keep continuity in their planning, building upon and learning from each meeting
- Help individual school community members develop their own skills
- Check frequently that all members understand the conversation, are abreast of ILT work and aware of decisions that have been made
- Come to consensus and make decisions collaboratively
- Find creative, constructive ways to resolve conflict
- Celebrate successes large and small

The ILT LEADS the entire school in:

- Challenging all community members in examining beliefs regarding the abilities of all students
- Analyzing school data and student work to identify strengths and opportunities for improvement
- Changing school structures to support the Instructional Focus
- Identifying and eliminating barriers to improvement
- Developing and implementing targeted professional development plans
- Involving faculty in strengthening professional relationships and networks

- Facilitating two-way communication between the ILT and other school community members
- Creating and implementing a whole school improvement plan focused on significant growth in student achievement

HOW THE ILT LIVES UP TO ITS NAME

Together with all members of the school community, the Instructional Leadership Team asks the following questions and engages in the following processes:

Instructional

- **Will this support the Instructional Focus and make a difference for students?** (Asks the critical questions and puts the structures in place to ensure that all school actions and conversations focus on this essential question.)
- **What do we know about how we are doing for students?** (Examines external and internal school data, student work, and classroom practices to identify strengths and opportunities for improvement.)
- **What SMARTe goals do we want for our students' achievement?** (Develops an inclusive process for determining the SMARTe goals and maintains these goals as the focus for all planning.)

Leadership

- **What is our vision for our students and our school?** (Engages all stakeholders in visioning and examining schoolwide beliefs and how they impact teaching and learning. Examines current conditions, including equity and access for all students.)
- **How do we get there?** (Creates a comprehensive school plan and utilizes it to change school structures to support improved student achievement. Develops understanding of the improvement process and *willing to challenge the status quo*.)

- **How do we know when we're there?** (Develops an internal accountability system to measure continued growth in student learning.)

Team

- **Who needs to be involved?** (Ensures that all school community members—families, school staff, faculty, administration, and students are included in the planning.)
- **What are our individual responsibilities?** (Learns from each other and across groups; accesses research data, training and experience; involves and informs others; is supportive, respectful, committed, focused, responsible, and reflective.)
- **How do we work together?** (Works openly, honestly, and collaboratively with shared leadership, responsibility, and trust. Tackles the tough issues; hears all viewpoints; develops creative, constructive ways to resolve conflict; maintains focus on vision of what is best for the students.)

Chapter 9

Lessons Learned about the Process of Improvement: Why Improve? Is It Possible? What Will It Take?

Why Improve?

Asking schools and school systems to improve dramatically is a pretty drastic request. It is often time consuming, painful, and expensive. Further, it suggests that the current practice is somehow deeply flawed. One could jump to the conclusion today's educators are not working hard enough or are simply not bright enough to get the results we are asking of them. Nothing could be further from the truth.

In reality, our current public schools are doing a wonderful job of what they were originally intended to do, perhaps even a better job than ever before. Our current public school system was envisioned some 150 years ago. At that time it was a great experiment. No other country in the world had the audacity to attempt to educate all of its children—even girls, even those whose families owned no property or titles, even those from different racial and ethnic backgrounds, and whose families spoke different languages.

At that time, the goal was to fully educate about 20 percent of the students, as that was the amount needed to go on for further training and education, to become the managers, leaders, and decision makers of the industrial society. The other 80 percent were to become literate to about the sixth grade level—the level at which newspapers and periodicals were written, as democracy requires an informed public. They were to be trained to follow directions and be comfortable performing routine tasks repeatedly for extended periods of time—skills needed in many industrial society jobs.

We would suggest public education is not only meeting this goal very well, but exceeding the goal by a great deal—significantly more than 20 percent are achieving full education and going on to advanced educational opportunities. Schools are accomplishing this with greater challenges than ever before, e.g. television, video games, chat rooms, and multiple organized sports; increased cultural and language diversity; and decreased parental involvement. Our schools and our educators should be celebrated for their success!

Unfortunately, while schools are excelling at meeting the old target for which they had been organized, the greater world has changed dramatically and the target has moved. The new world, the world of this century, is driven by a global economy and is an information-based society. The new target requires that **each** individual student be able to access information from a variety of sources—including the Internet—be able to organize, analyze, and use that information to make decisions, and to have sufficient communication skills to be able to explain and justify their decisions. That is to say that now 100 percent of the students must be fully educated and prepared to go on to further training throughout their lives. That is a formidable task and, as was stated earlier, schools have not been organized in such a way to accomplish this task. That is why educators must invest in the restructuring or reforming of educational practice and organization. In short, we have a new target; we must employ new strategies if we are to reach that target. Einstein's definition of insanity was to do the same thing over and over again and yet expect a different result. In public education, if we are to hit the new target, we must get very different results. That means we must do some different things, and we must do some of the same things differently.

Is It Possible?

The first question that comes up when we present this perspective is usually, "That sounds good, but is it even possible to fully educate all of our students?" There are three main reasons why we respond with an enthusiastic "Yes!" including (1) learning is natural—every human being learns, (2) formulating language is the most complex of cognitive activities—and nearly all children learn to do it fluently, and (3) we have lots of examples of schools and school systems where it is already happening.

The first support we cited is that learning is natural. We all know this is true and it might seem absurd to mention it here. But it is a very important point and a great strength in the favor of educators. There has been so much learned about how the brain functions and what some of the implications are about brain functioning and learning. Much of research supports the idea the brain is constantly creating meaning out of new experiences and information: organizing, categorizing, connecting to prior knowledge. All of this happens continuously—with or without the guidance of educators. The challenge then is not to figure out how to make some students learn—they are learning plenty all day long; but how to organize learning experiences so the learning is guided and developmental, and so those experiences match the learning styles or strategies of those children's brains. And we are learning more and more about just how to do that effectively.

The second support we cited for our belief that all students can become fully educated rests on the work of cognitive and social psychologists such as Jeff Howard. Jeff and his associates at the Efficacy Institute in Massachusetts have been trying to help us understand this for some time now. It seems formulating language—that is, being able to express feelings and ideas in words or being able to hold a spontaneous conversation—is the most complex of all cognitive activities. Any student who is capable of speaking a language fluently—any language—is capable of mastering everything we teach kindergarten through grade 12. It is so complicated that no computer can do it as well as a young child. In fact, it's so complicated that we don't fully understand how it works, how a child of two goes from, "hot, hot" to "may I please have a drink of water before I go to sleep or I'll scream." The brain makes sense and meaning through language, and almost all curriculum is delivered via language. This is true even if we consider advanced courses such as chemistry or calculus. Each is really a set of concepts expressed as specific terms and understanding or learning each is largely a matter of learning those terms and the relationships between them.

This is why we say, "any child who can speak a language—any language—is capable of mastering everything we teach K-12." It is understood some children never do learn to formulate language fluently, and may not be capable of mastering advanced curriculum, but this number is very, very small, usually estimated at under 4 percent of the students in our schools.

The third reason we give for our belief in the possibility of educating all students to high levels is perhaps the most convincing of all. We have an ever-increasing number of examples of places where educators have figured out how to do it! The work of James Stigler has pointed to whole countries, such as Japan or South Korea, and whole sections of Germany where all students are mastering the challenging curriculum provided. Recent publications highlight successful schools in the United States, as well. Doug Reeves talks about the ninety-ninety-ninety schools. Schools where 90 percent of the students come from families in poverty, where 90 percent of the students are ethnic or language minority, and where 90 percent of those students are literate at or above grade level standards. *No Excuses: Lessons from Twenty One High-Performing, High-Poverty Schools* is a book that presents twenty-one high-poverty, high-performing schools and draws some connections between them.

El Paso and Brazosport in Texas and Community District 2 in New York are districts with high poverty and high success rates. In addition, each of us at Focus on Results has been at a school that experienced similar high gains. One of us was a principal in a school in Southern California that moved from the eleventh percentile on the statewide tests to the ninety-plus percentiles in reading, math, and language. That school went from 80 percent Title I to where, if a student stayed at the school for two years, they could guarantee that the student would be on grade level and out of Title I. We believe firmly that all students can be fully educated because we have all been a part of a school where it happened.

Another important lesson we have learned is that there are reasons why more students are not learning to their full potential and reasons why more schools are not as successful as the models referred to above. One of those reasons is directly connected to the power of expectations. We will again defer to Jeff Howard and his powerful way of expressing this hurdle. The first point Jeff makes has to do with sorting. Many of us can remember that even as early as kindergarten, children are sorted for instruction. In many classes, there are the eagles, the robins, and the buzzards. It's great to be an eagle. It is really even okay to be a robin— you know you are not the smartest kid in the class but you are doing all right. Then there are the buzzards, and everyone in the class—including the buzzards—knows who they are.

Study after study shows kids live up to the expectations we set for them, and sure enough, most eagles stay eagles and most buzzards stay underperforming. There are lots of complex reasons for this, of course, but it's the sorting that starts it. Sadly, in urban settings, many of the children who end up in those buzzard groups are from ethnic and language minority groups. Jeff Howard, who is himself African American and passionate about the achievement gap between minority and white children, began his work with the assumption that this sorting was affecting primarily African American students—he was surprised to discover that this early and sustained sorting happens in all-white, suburban schools just as frequently. It doesn't stop there, though. Sorting is rampant in many junior and senior high schools, where counselors determine who will go on to college based on the classes they assign to students.

The Education Trust, under Katie Haycock, has put together some powerful statistics supporting this. Universities are notorious for sorting, even believing it is their responsibility, and it gets even worse at the graduate level. One of us began their doctoral studies with what was to be a cohort of thirty-nine students, all successful professional educators. After two quarters only nine remained, all of whom eventually earned their doctorates. The most common reason given by the other thirty who withdrew was, "I guess I am just not smart enough for this." It is a tragic loss when any person—child or adult—is allowed to believe they are not smart enough to accomplish something they want to do. Schools, parents, and the students themselves must all be helped to see that all students, with very, very few exceptions are completely capable of mastering our curriculum at high levels. The tool at the end of this chapter can be used as a way for a school or system to begin addressing this important issue.

Another reason for the failure of current public schools to meet the target of fully educating all students is linked to the organizational structure of our schools. It may at some point in the past have made sense to isolate classrooms where each teacher did what ever they thought best, but it certainly is not working now. Our collective experience strongly supports the work of Richard Elmore from Harvard University on this issue. He has suggested most schools and districts are run as loosely coupled systems with no clear tasks or accountability. He further suggests the current organization emphasizes management and *status quo* over leadership and improvement. All highly effective schools we have seen or studied have undergone a dramatic change in organization and organizational culture.

It is possible for schools and school systems to make the dramatic improvements in student learning we have been discussing. All it takes is intensive and sustained intervention using a systemic framework to guide the process. The following chapter outlines some of what we have learned about just what it will take to see dramatic improvement more often, in more settings.

TOOL FOR LEADERS

There are numerous anonymous slogans about the power of expectations, such as "Believing makes it so" or "If you think you can, you can. If you think you can't, you can't. You're right either way." In education, we still see many examples of places where low expectations for students go hand in hand with low performance and high expectations is directly connected to high performance. Part of the important foundational work involved in dramatically improving student performance in low performing settings is to raise the expectations of the teachers, the families, and the students themselves. There is a profound need to help all in the school and district community to begin to believe that high achievement by the great majority of students is indeed feasible.

The tool we found effective at beginning this conversation is the one we are including in this chapter. The strategy is simply to confront the participants—be they, principals, teachers, parents, community members—with examples of other places, with students and conditions similar to theirs, who have shown dramatic improvement in student performance and then ask the simple question, "If it could happen there, and there, and there, why not here?" Including input from sources like Jeff Howard can help participants understand the underlying reasons for the gains. The emphasis on this process is not on how these examples improved; that may come later. The emphasis is just on the fact that they did improve, that it truly is possible to attain such high goals. This tool includes a Facilitator's Guide and a Bibliography of potential articles and sources for examples of what is possible.

Examining Our Expectations Facilitator's Guide

Overview:

This activity uses specific questions given to the participants in advance to guide their thinking while reading an article and afterward to guide their discussion. Questions may need to be tailored to the content of the article for maximum effect. Attached is a simple example that has been used with our introductory presentation. If participants have the question guide during the activity, they can use it to take notes and jot questions that will inform the following discussion. This activity can also be used after a visit to a school or system that is being successful with "kids like ours."

Outcomes:

Participants will deepen their understanding of their expectations for student success.

Steps:

1. Provide participants with an overview of the activity.
2. Go over each question to be sure participants understand them and their use. Some sample questions might include:

   — What were the gains in student achievement for each example presented?
   — What were the students like in each example?
   — How is each example similar to our own setting? How is each different?

3. Introduce the article(s).

4. At the conclusion of the reading time, remind participants about the discussion questions, give them time parameters, and assign a facilitator for each group if needed.

5. Monitor the discussions and the time.

6. Midway through the discussion time, add a few questions such as these:

  — If it is possible in these settings, do you believe it is possible to see dramatic improvement in student learning here?
  — What might help us become one of these examples?

7. Conclude by reviewing key issues of how expectations can impact achievement and how this or a similar activity might be used in other settings to expand the conversation about expectations.

9.1 BIBLIOGRAPHY FOR BUILDING EXPECTATIONS THAT ALL STUDENTS CAN ACHIEVE AT HIGH LEVELS

The following represent some of the published material in the past few years that make it clear that ALL of our students are capable of mastering everything we teach K-12.

Title	Source	Information	Author	Supplier/Reference/Publisher
Annenberg Institute for Reform *www.studio.aisr.brown.edu*	Check this website.			
101 Questions & Answers about Standards, Assessment, and Accountability	book	90-90-90 Schools	Douglas B. Reeves	Advanced Learning Press Ph.: 800-844-6599 ISBN: 0-9644955-7-0 Amazon.com
Accountability in Action: A Blueprint for Learning	book	90-90-90 Schools: 90% free and reduced lunch, 90% minority students, 90% or more students who meet or exceed the state academic standards	Douglas B. Reeves	Amazon.com www.edaccountability.org
The 90% Reading Goal	book	a district that set and met a 3-year goal of 90% literacy	Lynn Fielding, Nancy Kerr, Paul Rosier	New Foundation Press 2527 W Kennewick Ave.#313 Kennewick, WA 99336 Ph.: 509-783-2139 Fax.: 509-783-5237 ISBN: 0-9666875-0-7 Amazon.com
www.edaccountability.org *www.edtrust.org*	Check these websites.			
High Student Achievement: How 6 School Districts Changed into High-Performing Systems	book		Gordon Cawelti and Nancy Prothance	Educational Resource Services www.ers.org Ph.: 703-243-2100 Ph.: 800-791-9308 Fax.: 703-243-1985 Stock #0420 ISBN 09705540-6-0
No Excuses: Lessons from 21 High-performing, High-poverty Schools	book	90% free and reduced lunch, 90% minority students, 90% or more students who meet or exceed the state academic standards	Samuel Casey Carter	The Heritage Foundation 214 Massachusetts Ave., NE Washington DC 2002-4999 *www.heritage.org* ISBN: 0-89195-090-7 Amazon.com
The Right to Learn: A Blueprint for Creating Schools that Work	book		Linda Darling Hammond (1997)	www. Amazon.com
Getting Smart: The Social Construction of Intelligence	article		Jeff Howard	Efficacy Institute Waltham, Mass. 781-547-6060

Chapter 10

Accelerating the Improvement Agenda: Districtwide Improvement Initiatives

Throughout this book, we have discussed strategies by which districts may support school implementation in each area of our framework. However, it is worth discussing a districtwide approach to school improvement.

We know it is possible to see improvement one school at a time—each of us worked as a principal where the school made dramatic gains in student achievement despite the fact that the larger district was not involved in systemic improvement initiatives. We also know, however, that because of the great work involved, the slowness of the pace and the fragile nature of gains made, the most lasting improvement efforts must be rooted in a districtwide approach to systemic improvement.

Over the past ten years, a great amount of federal money has been put into single school reform via the Comprehensive School Reform Program. In this program, schools selected a "proven model" based on a range of research options and then adopted the beliefs and practices of that model. Schools received anywhere from $50,000 to $75,000 per year, for three to five years to learn and implement these models. Even though there are thousands of these schools nationwide, very few of them have demonstrated dramatic improvement in student learning as a result of adopting their model. This may be partially the fault of the models but it is more likely that adoption of a model in isolation of ongoing district requirements, policies, and practices results in low-level implementation and confusing results at the site level.

Instead, we have seen very broad and fairly timely improvements in even large districts when everyone is working together to support the work of the schools around strategic implementation. We have worked in districts with as few as five schools and as many as 209 schools, yet in all situations where leadership at all levels was committed to success, we have seen significant improvements in both instructional practice and student performance within two years. Since the whole system is working toward the support of effective instruction, districtwide practices and policies have changed along with site practices, greatly increasing the likelihood of having those gains last over time. It is essential to shift the emphasis from individual school-based models to districtwide approaches.

The following is intended to help superintendents and their cabinet begin to consider where they are in relation to where they want to be and strategize how they might refocus a traditional Central Office into a results-oriented, instruction-focused, and customer-service-driven organization called Central Services.

From Central Offices . . .

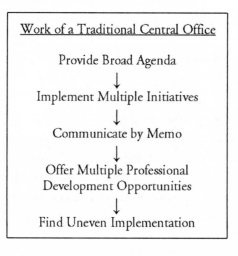

The work of a traditional Central Office often flows down in a linear fashion. The district begins by providing a broad improvement agenda and then develops multiple initiatives to help schools implement the agenda. Central Offices communicate these ideas through numerous memos to schools and offer multiple and sometimes competing professional development opportunities to support implementation of the various initiatives. Most traditional Central Offices expect learning to improve out of this process. However, they often find that implementation of these plans and initiatives is uneven across the schools.

When traditional Central Office staffs accept this process as the status quo, not surprisingly, so do district principals, teachers, and of course, students. The typical school staff ends up believing the Central Office is out of touch with their true needs. A recent survey of school leaders by Burch suggests schools are frustrated that Central Office staff rarely visit their buildings to see school challenges first hand, much less ask schools to define their hurdles, strategies, and needs. Communication from the Central Office tends to be directive instead of engaging and reciprocal. Schools perceive district personnel to have a poor grasp of teaching and learning and therefore incapable of truly supporting their needs.

This research suggests a disconnect between district intent and school understanding and implementation. To reconcile this challenge, districts must be willing to improve side-by-side with their schools.

. . . To Central Services

We support districts in moving from a traditional Central Office to a Central Services organization sharply focused on instruction. By this, we mean rethinking the way district staff see their responsibilities, tools, expectations, strategies, interactions, and even their name. The purpose of this revamped Central Services is to provide high-quality customer service to its primary constituent, schools. Success of Central Services is defined not by compliance of schools, but by the support to and achievements of the schools in achieving results for students.

Work of Central Services

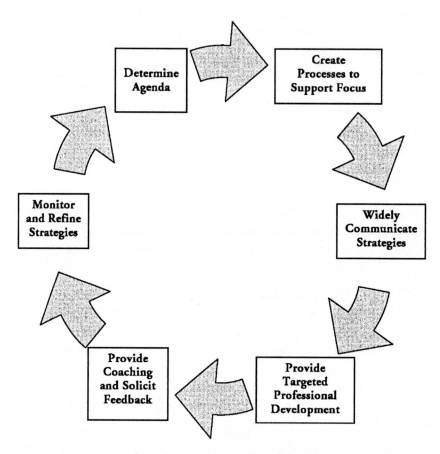

In Central Services, the work of the district evolves from a linear to a circular flow. When developing agendas, strategies, and professional development offerings, Central Services solicits feedback from its clients—the schools—to ensure the district is in fact serving their needs.

For example, the Superintendent in Edmonton, Alberta led his Central Office to develop into a Central Services organization by ensuring his administration truly supported the needs of his schools. He created the districtwide focus of achieving "superb results from all students" and asked each department within Edmonton Central Services to define its work by how it will support such student results. Further, he provided district staff with the professional development they needed to reframe their work and become more customer-service oriented.

GETTING STARTED

Moving from a traditional Central Office to Central Services often requires rethinking the way districts do business. For example, look at the new way Central Services does its old job as detailed below. Reflecting on your own district, where does it fall on this continuum? What specific examples support your placement? What are the next steps you can take to move your district toward the Central Services side of the continuum?

Work at the District Level		
From Central Office...	→	To Central Services
Provide broad agenda for improvement.	→	Use student data to develop a focused district improvement plan.
Implement multiple initiatives designed to improve achievement.	→	Create and use policies, practices, and resources that are aligned to support the district-wide improvement agenda.
Send frequent memos to outline schools' compliance.	→	Widely communicate district strategies and student learning goals.
Offer multiple and sometimes competing professional development opportunities.	→	Provide targeted professional development based on school and district needs.
Find uneven implementation of various initiatives.	→	Provide follow-up coaching, solicit feedback from schools, and monitor student progress toward stated goals to help ensure all schools meet district expectations.

Use student data to develop focused district improvement plan.

Central Services develops a district improvement agenda first by determining the true needs of the schools throughout the district and then developing a plan to address those specific needs.

Central Services determines its schools' needs by examining multiple sources of data including standardized tests, local performance-based assessments, and samples of student work. Central Services also solicits input from school leaders by surveying their greatest strengths and challenges and asking how the district may better support their needs. Forums for gathering this information might include focus groups, satisfaction surveys, and regular conversations with schools.

Based on this data, Central Services determines its schools' greatest need. Our experience suggests districts should support schools in identifying one specific Instructional Focus—one area of the academic curriculum the staff has chosen as most important for its students to know and do. Finally, the district builds an improvement agenda that directly addresses this most pressing student need and instructs all Central Services staff to reorganize their daily work to support the Instructional Focus.

One district in Washington State reorganized the work of every department to support the districtwide focus on literacy. For example, the Transportation Department refocused its efforts by placing boxes of books on each bus for students to read while riding to and from school. They even redesigned their bus safety presentations around characters from popular children's stories.

Create and use policies, practices, and resources that are aligned to support the districtwide improvement agenda.

Central Services takes great care to translate the districtwide agenda into reflective and helpful tools, policies, and practices that directly support each school's Instructional Focus. One Central Services provided schools with access to evidence-based teaching practices by developing a districtwide database that included literature, materials, and tools to help each school implement its Instructional Focus.

In addition, these districts reallocate their resources including time, personnel, and funding to ensure these assets align with the focus of the schools. One district returned control of professional development time to the schools so that teachers could collaborate within the regular work day and support each other in their Instructional Focus. Another Central Services streamlined the teacher application process to assume increased responsibility and free more time for principals to visit classrooms.

Finally, Central Services make student learning outcomes the only bottom line that matters. It is only when these practices are fully implemented every day, in every classroom, for every student, at every school, that we can expect to see dramatic improvement in student learning. It is only when every person in the system is truly spending their time supporting and holding accountable those teachers that we can expect them to be able to deliver high quality instruction every day. Then we will see improvement in student learning, and only then can we know what we are doing is working. We fully believe in the value of celebrating incremental success and certainly some of those increments involve adult behaviors. We just want to be very clear the only value in changes in adult behavior is when those changes result in improvement in student learning; that is the only real bottom line.

Widely communicate district strategies and student learning goals.

By widely communicate, we mean do it repeatedly, and in a way that is helpful and easy to access at the school level. Central Services communicates using words, actions, and deeds in every available forum. Each time the superintendent speaks, he or she details the agenda and strategy for improvement. Wherever Central Services staff work, these ideas are displayed shamelessly throughout the building. As one superintendent said, "when my staff interrupts me saying, 'I know, I know, our agenda is . . . ,' then I know I am communicating the strategies enough." Another Central Services organization posts the district agenda throughout their building, including on the elevators, on each table in the district cafeteria, on signs in the parking deck—even on the recorded phone message heard while holding for a district staff member.

School faculty do not have time to attend weekly meetings at the district office, complete the reams of paperwork that comes their way, or truly digest the implementation strategies laid out in a memo. Instead, Central Services reduces the amount of paperwork sent to schools, reserving that right for truly important information that cannot be communicated any other way. One district met this challenge by compiling a chronological list of all the district requests made to schools and then cutting the list by 50 percent.

Provide targeted professional development based on school and district needs.

Traditional Central Offices offer a wide range of professional development opportunities that may be disconnected from the Instructional Focus or even compete with other districtwide initiatives. Central Services supports schools in creating a targeted professional development plan based on student needs.

For example, one district tied its professional development to each school's needs by providing training in walk-throughs. This powerful tool enabled faculties to learn how to visit others' classrooms to learn from and provide support to colleagues as they implemented their Instructional Focus.

Professional development is not an offering simply for schools. Central Services staff needs professional development, too. In one district, Central Services provided a series of professional development sessions to its staff to examine how the district's improvement agenda impacted their own daily work.

Provide follow-up coaching, solicit feedback from schools, and monitor student progress toward stated goals to help ensure all schools meet district expectations.

After professional development workshops are completed, traditional Central Offices hope their hard work pays off at the school level and that student learning improves. In Central Services, professional development sessions are followed up with more than hope. Instead, these districts provide school-level coaching to ensure the training translates into practice. The most successful models usually involve a cadre of coaches who provide ongoing phone, e-mail, and on-site visits to help the leadership team apply its new learnings in the workplace.

In conjunction with the ongoing coaching, Central Services also develops and uses a system to solicit feedback from schools and monitor student progress toward district goals. It sets performance targets by which Central Services staff may measure its own effectiveness throughout the year. For example, one Central Services department set the following external performance target, "98 percent of principals will be satisfied or very satisfied with the services provided to them by Personnel Services as noted on the annual District Satisfaction Survey."

This specific data enables Central Services to refine its strategies and provide better customer service to its schools. For example, principals gave one district the feedback that they were unable to spend time in classrooms because of daily district requests and demands. In response, the district committed to holding all communications to schools until after 10:00 a.m., enabling principals to use this sacred time for instructional leadership.

Finally, the superintendent and cabinet clearly define expectations for implementation of the district effort and hold schools increasingly accountable for using these strategies in the classroom.

Challenges to Districtwide Improvement

There are numerous challenges to addressing whole systems rather than individual schools yet the effects seem worth the effort. One critical factor is the engagement of the superintendent. We have found the day-to-day work of many superintendents is quite removed from effective instructional practice and the type of leadership that supports it. However, we have also seen when superintendents actively support and participate in a districtwide initiative to promote quality instruction and instructional leadership amazing things happen.

It is also interesting to note that by all appearances, it is actually quite possible for a superintendent to be fully engaged in significant transformation and still keep their job. It seems results in student learning counts heavily with many school boards, outweighing complaints about the difficulty of change that often come from some district staff.

Central Offices pose a challenge to systemic reform because they often require restructuring or retraining to become support systems rather than directive systems and because they need to work more collaboratively—with each other as well as with the schools—to be able to be as responsive as they need to be. Central Services personnel are an essential part of the support and accountability link in a systemwide effort to improve instruction and student learning, but few of them are provided sufficient freedom and clarity of purpose to be able to accomplish their intent in isolated units and departments.

Another challenge to systemwide improvement is that each school in a district is a unique culture and is at its own individual spot in the journey to full effectiveness. Any training must be sufficiently differentiated to allow for recognition of each site's strengths and yet challenge each site to move forward in other areas. In each case this must include clear expectations for implementation to ensure the training translates to concrete action in the workplace.

This is partially why it is essential to have a coaching piece in the improvement initiative to best support this individualization. In districts using the FOR framework, each building principal and many central service leaders have a coach that meets with him or her on a regular basis to reflect together on how the work is being implemented. Following our structured Results-Based Coaching model, this individualized time allows each participant to progress at their own rate, but with built in accountability and support for the implementation process.

Despite the challenges, we have found whole district improvement is more than just possible; it is in some ways easier and certainly more efficient in achieving the gains desired and having them sustained over time. Given the scope of need in most urban settings across our country, it seems also essential to look more broadly than one school at a time, and to focus on deep systemwide improvements.

Sucessful districts focus foundation and additional government funding on systemic efforts.

One of the major issues of recent years is the reluctance of the prevailing culture to focus foundation and government grant efforts around comprehensive frameworks for improving student learning; that is frameworks that address developing the capacity of leadership at all levels, developing the instructional knowledge and skills of both administrators and teachers to high levels of mastery, and developing support and monitoring systems that assure full implementation of those instructional practices in every classroom, every day, for every student.

Instead, we have foundations that focus on leadership training, charter schools, small secondary schools, middle grades models, individual school reform, or a host of other sub-categories. It is not clear why this inclination toward a particular niche is so prevalent. Certainly foundations have their own aims and guiding principles; they often hope to gain public recognition for their parent company or founding family, or they have a leader with a personal bias or interest in one aspect of the work, and that then becomes the focus for them. Federal and state grants must be approved by a wide range of interested parties, so those programs often state very specific targets in order to gain legislative approval.

These may be some of the reasons we see so much money being spent in such a piecemeal fashion, seldom generating dramatic improvements in student learning. In this time of economic challenge, local schools and school systems rarely have sufficient funds to seek the comprehensive help they need and want. To really accelerate the improvement agenda, much more money targeted for school improvement, both by private foundations and government grants, must be allocated to comprehensive, systemic improvement, directly tied to specific student learning goals as the only measure of true success.

This is actually a very achievable goal. We have had the privilege of working with several foundations over the past few years that have embraced a comprehensive approach and together we saw exciting results for children. The foundation at Walt Disney Studios, currently called Disney Hand, moved beyond their annual Teacher of the Year award show to sponsor the Creative Learning Communities (CLC) program from 1999 to 2002. Thirty schools grouped in seventeen projects were identified across the country as having improvement plans based on creative teaching methods, which fit Disney's profile as one of the most creative organizations in the world. However, instead of just funding the projects and highlighting the creative teaching, the CLC staff brought in Focus on Results to co-develop and conduct an intensive series of leadership workshops over three years that helped each of the projects connect their creative teaching approaches to measurable goals and assessments of student learning. The program was a huge success, with each of the projects reaching full implementation of their strategies and often surpassing the challenging goals for student learning they had set.

We have also been working with the Ball Foundation of Glen Ellyn, Illinois, for the past three years. This work was begun in Chula Vista,

California, and has since expanded to include Springfield, Illinois. In each of these districts, we are collaborating with the foundation and the school system to work with the comprehensive framework in small groups of schools over three years, adding schools each year to achieve a tipping point where the district capacity is developed to such a degree they are then able to continue the work themselves with their remaining schools. Again, the gains in student learning are very powerful. The Ball Foundation is an excellent example of an organization committed to improving student achievement; they have tried several approaches to make this happen and are now finding the results they have been seeking by using the comprehensive framework.

The Broad Foundation partnered with the *Los Angeles Times* and Focus on Results to apply our framework at fifty schools in Southern California as part of the Reading by Nine initiative. The individual schools involved were so successful it has led several districts to expand the program districtwide. The Stupski Family Foundation engaged Focus on Results to work on systemwide improvement with several districts as well.

These are just a few examples of foundations we have worked with who were willing to expand their previous niche to include a comprehensive framework approach directly tied to student learning. There have been powerful gains as a result of each of those partnerships. We strongly encourage other foundations to support technical assistance for districts using a comprehensive framework in order to achieve the impact on student learning they seek and to accelerate the overall improvement agenda.

We have also worked in a few settings where schools or systems were clever enough to figure out how to pool Comprehensive School Reform Grants to build on the system's strengths rather than having each site adopt an independent and often conflicting model. These situations, like New Bedford, Massachusetts, have all proven to have a positive impact on the whole system as well as each participating school. Federal and state grants would do well to follow the model of funding inclusive, systemwide reform based on a comprehensive framework rather than supporting scattered projects that rarely impact student learning and even more rarely become institutionalized as part of the greater system. New Jersey is an example of a state that has recently begun to shift from single school to systemic support for improvement.

Districts should capitalize on the power of external partnerships.

When we were principals working to improve our own schools we were largely on our own, trying to figure out what to do next. When we met and shared our stories, however, it was interesting that each of us had somehow connected with an external partnership that both strengthened and deepened our work. For two of us it was the National Paideia Center, where working with other schools to implement the Socratic Method of questioning to build critical thinking skills helped us see what others were wrestling with, provided a new source of ideas and a supportive source of encouragement and reinforcement about what had been done that was working. For another it was the Harvard University Principals Center, where semi-annual planning workshops and summer institutes kept up a constant flow of new ideas and a national range of perspectives. For the other it was having a coach from UCLA who visited the school weekly and provided feedback and support. Each of us credits these external partnerships as contributing in powerful ways to our leadership and to the improvement in student learning we saw at our schools.

In our work as Focus on Results, we are the external partnership with most of our school systems, and we continue to hear frequently how helpful it is to have someone come in from outside the system to look with fresh eyes and give specific feedback on what we see. Sometimes the feedback is in the form of questions, "Why do you?" Often the answer is, "I don't know why, we've just always done it that way." Then we are able to collaborate to find a more effective or efficient way. Sometimes the feedback is just mirroring what we see. When we say it everyone in the room suddenly sees it too, as if for the first time.

For example, we were recently at a district in the middle of its second year of a systemwide focus on literacy. As part of our meeting, we pointed out even with their stated focus on literacy, all the student work displayed at their district office was student art—with no writing attached, sending a very different message about what they truly valued. Everyone in the room instantly saw their district messaging in a new light. Sometimes the feedback we give is just supportive of good practices we see; it is always amazing how little appreciation hard working educators receive, and many times it is the first time someone has been told how well they are doing and how much better shape they are in than other districts. Always, the feedback is tied to the student learning goals the school or system has set, and even when the feedback is somewhat critical of current practice, it is received with appreciation by the educators committed to those goals.

Because of the power we have seen in external partnerships, we strongly encourage any school or school system serious about improvement to identify a way to engage external eyes to give feedback about the work and to ask hard questions about the process. Many situations are well served to partner with an external technical assistance provider, such as Focus on Results, that can provide direct assistance in identifying or developing a guiding comprehensive framework and then provide training and coaching to help develop the capacity to fully implement improvements. Some settings may not require that much in-depth help; for those settings, there are many other sources for external partnering as well, including leaders from other school systems, universities, technical assistance providers, local government, and business. It is important to be very clear about what the role of the partner is to be, for their benefit as well as your own, and to tie that role very closely to student learning. University and business-based partnership programs often have objectives in mind for the benefit of the partner rather than for the sole benefit of the school or school system. Being clear up front can save time and increase value throughout the life of the partnership. The really important thing is to remember that progress can be defined only through significant results in student learning, not by the number of illustrious external partnerships one has been able to form.

Successful districts establish regular opportunities for technical assistance providers to meet and share strategies and practices that are producing results.

We at Focus on Results have had the opportunity over the past ten years to work with numerous other organizations that provide technical assistance to schools and school systems, and we have learned from each of them. The UCLA School Management Program, the Boston Plan for Excellence, the National Paideia Center, the Association of California School Administrators, Harvard University Principals Center, the Achievement Council, ATLAS, the National Middle Schools Forum, and the Education Development Center (EDC) in Newton, Massachusetts are among those that helped shape our work and to whom we owe a debt of gratitude. Hopefully, members of those organizations will say that we also contributed to their knowledge base and practice. However, such sharing opportunities are rare and often informal rather than systematic.

As stated several times earlier, the purpose of writing this book is to further open the conversation about what works in school improvement. It is our hope that these ideas will indeed contribute to strengthening the work of other technical assistance providers as well. It seems all those who have committed their lives to improving the learning opportunities for children are willing to share and help others help the children.

Something more is needed, however, than what we are doing now. The learning curve is too low and the learning rate is too slow. Our final suggestion is to convene a conversation for technical assistance providers that would allow open sharing of strategies, frameworks, materials, and perspectives, and hopefully lead to ongoing informal connections and communication via Internet, articles, books, etcetera. The format might be fairly structured, like the Conversations for the International Network of Principal Centers, or it might be more flexible, as with Open Space Technology. It might be a separate event or it might be combined with some organization's annual conference, such as ASCD. To be truly effective at meeting the huge challenge of having universally successful schools, where each student is achieving at high standards, we must find more ways to work together. We will only be as strong as we need to be when all of us know what each of us knows.

Chapter 11

Focus on Results: How We Can Help

Throughout this book, we have discussed a detailed framework to guide school leaders in using data to support improved student learning. Based on our work implementing this framework in the field over the last ten years, Focus on Results (FOR) has developed specific technical assistance offerings to support educators implementing the framework in their schools and districts.

Focus on Results is a consulting group of highly experienced teachers, principals, and central office staff that have led schools and districts to post significant gains in student learning. Our expert practitioners provide technical assistance to both schools and districts in implementing the Seven Areas of Focus. We are based throughout North America and bring one hundred plus years of experience working in and with schools and districts.

Cookie-cutter initiatives and "off the shelf" improvement models just don't work. Instead of trying to implement one-size-fits-all canned solutions, we tailor our approach based on what we learn about each district and school. We work to identify local needs and develop a technical assistance plan that we think will work best for each individual school and district environment.

FOR offers four strands of such technical assistance:

1. Executive Coaching for Superintendent and Cabinet

2. Training for Central Office Leadership
3. Training for School-Based Leadership
4. Systems Study

1. Executive Coaching For Superintendent and Cabinet

Executive coaching is an ongoing professional relationship that helps senior leaders produce extraordinary results in their organizations. With coaching provided by the Focus on Results team of expert practitioners, leaders deepen their learning, improve their performance, and enhance the quality of their professional lives.

FOR provides coaching to superintendents and their cabinet members to help them to

- Provide leadership for strategic pressure and support in all areas of the organization;
- Use strong student assessment data to drive decisions and set clear, measurable student learning goals;
- Provide ongoing professional development at all levels of the system that builds true expertise and leads to full implementation of systemwide evidence-based instructional practices;
- Apply intentional instructional leadership at all levels to ensure expectations are met; and
- Hold accountable all central office departments to be in direct support of teaching and learning.

What Does It Look Like?

Focus on Results Executive Coaching centers around issues critical to leading and supporting improvement in student learning within the district. FOR coaches meet with the superintendent and cabinet, both separately and together to provide support and feedback as they work together to achieve results. Both the FOR coach and the group generate topics for these discussions collaboratively. Participants set specific goals for each session; detail follow-up between sessions; plan strategies and tactics for collaboration, decision making, and implementation; and develop accountability structures.

How Much Time Does It Take?

Coaching sessions are usually about an hour long and seem to yield the best results when held at least monthly. Distance coaching via phone and email takes place between regular coaching sessions. In addition, FOR coaches offer full or multi-day retreats for long-range strategic planning and focused team building.

Example

FOR partnered with Edmonton Public Schools to develop an executive coaching strategy that includes the following components.

Features of the Edmonton / FOR Executive Coaching Work

1. *Monthly "in briefs" for superintendent to share plans and ideas for FOR work and "out briefs" for FOR to share the learning, updates, and suggestions with superintendent.*
2. *Together, partners evaluate progress of the district's improvement agenda and strategize on leadership tactics needed to keep student achievement agenda as the "main thing."*
3. *Assess strengths and weaknesses of each cabinet member and strategize on steps needed to support and improve their individual work.*
4. *Plan collectively with the cabinet each month.*
5. *Provide support to cabinet including basic team development; meeting structure and facilitation; decision making; and the use of accountability structures (for example, a to-do list.)*
6. *Plan and facilitate quarterly cabinet retreats.*

---

2. Training for Central Office Leadership

FOR also works with the Central Office Leadership—department heads and division leaders—to help them implement the framework. FOR supports central office leadership to help them

- Ensure district student learning goals for improving teaching and learning and student performance are widely communicated and drive everything;
- Create and use plans, policies, programs, practices, and resources that are aligned to support school improvement and staff collaboration at all levels;
- Ensure every central office department is performance and customer service driven and strives for continuous improvement;
- Expect the district to act as a customer service provider to meet school and central office professional development needs; and
- Create an easily accessible, user-friendly student data system that supports ongoing program evaluation and continuous improvement by staff at all levels.

What does it look like?

FOR meets with department heads to discuss the superintendent and cabinet's goals for the district and discuss how the Central Office Leadership can effectively translate these goals into supportive policies and practices for the schools. FOR provides professional development sessions for Central Office personnel and meets with department leaders separately and collectively to address individual needs and coordinate strategies both within and across departments.

Setting Clear expectations for Implementation

After initial training sessions, FOR works with Central Office Leaders to set expectations for implementation. FOR has developed a comprehensive set of expectations that are adjusted to meet local needs. Both Central Office Leaders and FOR agree on these expectations before moving forward to launch the partnership with a clear understanding of responsibilities, roles, and goals.

Coaching for Central Office Leaders

After initial training and setting of expectations, FOR provides ongoing coaching to Central Office Leaders to support them in implementing the framework. Coaches support these Leaders through onsite visits, phone calls, and emails as they try new practices to become more customer-driven and focused on supporting school and district improvement.

3. Training for School-Based Leadership

FOR also provides direct support to leaders in schools—principals and Instructional Leadership Teams (ILTs)—to support the implementation of the Seven Areas of Focus. Depending on the school, FOR may work with the principal and one teacher leader, or the principal and an entire ILT with as many as ten people. Again, FOR works according to local needs and context.

FOR begins by providing an initial kick-off training to schools within the district that includes concrete strategies to use when they return to their buildings. These sessions are interactive, content-driven, and provide practical, hands on tools so that principals and ILTs may directly apply their learning to their daily work.

FOR then provides half and full-day monthly meetings to schools where they follow up on the "homework" the participants received. FOR provides support to and accountability for leaders as they implement these strategies.

FOR also builds in training on sustainability and building internal capacity so that principals and ILTs may take on this work themselves with time.

FOR school partnerships last an average of three years, and include a concrete plan to build in-house capacity to help the framework become "the way we do things here."

Setting Clear Expectations for Implementation

FOR has developed a set of comprehensive core expectations for implementation that are adapted with each of our partner schools to fit the needs and goals of that building. These expectations will not only give FOR and the schools a concrete guide by which to move forward, but will also provide a rubric by which to measure progress.

For example, a set of districtwide Expectations for Implementation from one of our partner districts is as follows. We work with school leaders to translate these expectations into action to meet the expectations.

Example: Districtwide Expectations for School Implementation

1. **Deepen the Implementation of the District and Schoolwide Literacy Focus**

There is obvious evidence that the school is "living" a solid schoolwide focus on equity-based literacy through its words, actions, and deeds. There is evidence of how the district is supporting the equity-based literacy efforts at the school sites.

2. **Develop Professional Collaboration Teams to Improve Teaching and Learning**

Using protocols and strategies, teacher teams meet regularly to talk about student work, teacher assignments, effective literacy practices, and data that demonstrate progress toward eliminating the achievement gap. The principal participates in these meetings. These meetings drive improvements in teaching and learning. The

---

Instructional Leadership Team meets regularly and is providing strong leadership around the schoolwide focus on equity-based literacy.

3. Learn and Use Effective Evidence-Based Programs

Progress is being made at schoolwide implementation of the District's language arts adoption program (best literacy practices) in each and every classroom, for each and every student—including African Americans and Hispanics—each and every day.

4. Implement a Targeted Professional Development Plan That Builds Expertise in Selected Programs (Evidence-Based Practices) and Addresses the Achievement Gap

The school's professional development supports the focus on equity-based literacy by building teacher expertise through literacy training and promoting high expectations for all students including African American and Hispanics. As expertise is developed, teachers are held increasingly accountable for implementation of standards-based, district-selected, equity-based literacy programs.

5. Realign Resources (People, Time, Talent, Energy, and Money) to Support the Instructional Focus

The school can demonstrate clear evidence that the Instructional Leadership Team is guiding school decisions about the use of all its resources.

6. Engage Families and the Community in Supporting the Instructional Focus

The school can demonstrate clear evidence that it is involving families, including the families of African American and Hispanic students, and the community with the schoolwide equity-based literacy focus.

7. SMARTe (Specific, Measurable, Attainable and challenging, Relevant, Timely, and touch every student) Goals

The school has met at least two schoolwide SMARTe goals. One is in relation to the statewide standardized test and the other is in relation to a local measure of student performance as per the standards-based, district-adopted, equity-based literacy program. Results are easily available and publicly posted. The data is part of an internal accountability system that is used by the Instructional Leadership Team as a lens for decision making.

8. Principal as Instructional Leader

The principal is meeting the goal of spending 50 percent of the instructional day in classrooms—observing, demonstrating, modeling, and supporting effective implementation of the standards-based, district-selected, equity-based literacy program and supporting the use of evidence-based practices across the content areas.

Coaching for School-Based Leadership

Research clearly indicates that professional development is most effective when it is embedded within teachers' day-to-day jobs and ongoing with frequent opportunities for coaching and practice. While school leaders often attend excellent, motivating—yet isolated—training events, these isolated events rarely translate into improved practice. School leaders need ongoing support, site visits, and leadership coaching to support their efforts at turning the training into concrete actions on-site.

FOR provides a cadre of experienced coaches who are assigned to each of the ILTs. These coaches not only provide training events, but offer ongoing phone, e-mail and on-site visits to help the leadership team apply its new learnings in the workplace. Coaching visits are regular, with the first one scheduled after the initial training. They then take place between each session to help teams stay focused and on-target in their plans, and to implement what they have learned.

4. Systems Study

A Systems Study is a confidential, in-depth examination of all aspects of a school district: from policy to personnel, from communication to curriculum, from leadership to libraries, and all stops in between. A Focus on Results systems audit helps a school district know whether its programs, staffing, policies, and procedures are ready to support a districtwide focus on improving student performance, and to support principals spending more time as instructional leaders.

The systems audit is designed to address these three questions:

- What is the district culture for improvement?
- What is the impact of programs, policies, and standard operating procedures on a districtwide focus on improving student performance and principals spending more time as instructional leaders?
- What is the district's readiness to lead improvement with its central office?

The findings of this audit can help guide the improvement efforts by the superintendent, central office staff, and the school principals. Focus on Results works with districts after an audit is completed to help develop recommendations; provide professional development to central office staff, principals, and their leadership teams; and to provide a system of follow-up and on-site executive coaching.

The methodology for conducting the systems audit involves data collection, data analysis/synthesis, and report writing. We organize our specific findings around the three areas that guide our perspective on assessing central office capacity and support for improving student performance in schools:

1. What central offices do to help schools improve performance,
2. What schools do to significantly improve performance, and
3. How organizations lead successful transformation efforts.

For each of the key elements in the three areas, we have identified a set of indicators that we would expect to see in place in a district that has fully implemented these elements. We indicate for each element whether we think the indicators are present, partially present, or absent, and what the evidence is that supports our assessments.

We summarize our conclusions for each element or set of elements, and for the first and second areas, suggest short—and long-term opportunities for the district to consider.

The collaborative process compares all findings with a framework for successful systems integration and leads to the identification of, and an intervention plan for, several priority growth areas.

Why do it?

An increasing amount of research on school improvement is highlighting the need for districtwide systemic reform as opposed to targeting only individual schools. The work of Richard Elmore, from Harvard University, has identified the loosely coupled systems organization of most schools and school districts as one of the leading challenges to significant, lasting school improvement. Ten years of attempting to implement school "models" has shown that many isolated school interventions fail, while those that succeed often slip back if they are not a part of an improving district. The resulting message is that only by aligning all district systems and resources to support the improvements needed in teaching and learning can we expect to see lasting growth in student achievement.

The timing of a systems audit depends on the districts. Some districts wish to dive directly into implementing the framework, learning about systemic needs as it goes. Other districts would rather look at the whole system first, before engaging in the work. Either strategy works. It simply depends on the needs and desires of the district leaders.

What about local context?

The entire systems study is a collaborative process. A local guiding coalition of local leaders is set up from the very beginning to tailor the design of the study to integrate into the local setting. The type of data to collect, the processes for collecting the data, what documents to review, whom to interview, how many and which priorities to identify are all determined together. Recommendations for improvement are based on the framework, and the plan for building capacity to implement the recommendations are all designed collaboratively with local context and culture in mind.

Next Steps

For more information on how Focus on Results might support your school or district, please visit our website at *www.focusonresults.net* or contact us at

for@focusonresults.net

West Coast

Focus on Results
5901 Warner Avenue, #441
Huntington Beach, CA 92649
Phone: 888 743 1076
Fax: 508 869 0562

East Coast

Focus on Results
198 Tremont Street, #408
Boston, MA 02116-4705
Phone: 888 743 1076
Fax: 508 869 0562

Appendix A

Results Summary

At Focus on Results, we monitor both implementation and student achievement data closely, not only to measure our own success, but to refine strategies to meet the specific needs of our partners throughout North America. The data from our partner districts and schools show that our work is making a positive impact on the only bottom line that matters—student achievement.

Because of the nature of data reporting and the need to continuously update achievement results each year, we refrain from including this information in this book and instead have posted it on our website at *www.focusonresults.net/results*. Here you will find a comprehensive examination of the most up-to-date student achievement data from our partner districts including

- a summary of the scope of work with each district,
- a snapshot of the district including demographic and socioeconomic information of its students, and
- pre- and post-intervention student achievement scores, with comparison groups where applicable.

We will continually update the website as more information becomes available to ensure the reader has access to the continued progress of our partner students, schools, and districts.

Appendix B

Evidence and Research Base

Over the last ten years of implementation of the Focus framework, is has been clear to the hundreds of practitioners that have implemented it with fidelity that "this stuff works." Results have improved and districts have been satisfied that their investment of time and resources is paying off.

In addition, participants sometimes ask to review the relevant educational research that supports the professional knowledge base behind the Focus framework. For many, working from a research base brings credibility to the work as well as provides a wider context about the work that schools and districts are undertaking. Also, having an opportunity to share and discuss what was tried in other districts and the research related to it often provides an opportunity for school and district leaders to gain a deeper understanding of their local context, staff skills and abilities, as well as both successful and challenging initiatives.

To help further those discussions, we have created the attached appendix. It includes a brief summary of relevant research and an extended bibliography of research that connects to each of the seven Areas of the framework.

Area 1: Identify and Implement a Schoolwide Instructional Focus

A 1995 Research Synthesis on Effective Schooling Practices by Kathleen Cotton at the Northwest Regional Educational Laboratory[1] states that a key finding in the literature is that in highly effective schools, "everyone in the school community emphasizes the importance of learning" and that "administrators and teachers emphasize academic achievement when setting goals and school policies and focus on student learning considerations as the most important criteria for making decisions."

The U.S. Department of Education's monograph, Turning Around Low-Performing Schools: A Guide for State and Local Leaders (May 1998)[2] emphasizes a focus on learning as an important strategy for improving student achievement. The monograph cited a 1997 study of twenty-six high-achieving, high-poverty schools in Texas that found effective schools exhibited similar characteristics, including "a strong focus on ensuring academic success for each student and a refusal to accept excuses for poor performance."

Another study cited in the monograph is a 1997 study by Hawley, et al, on successful high-poverty schools in Maryland.[3] The authors attribute improvements in reading to a number of factors, including a focus on reading across the entire school.

In Southern California, researchers from UCLA worked with fifteen K-5 schools and serve predominantly poor and working-class Hispanic communities from 1997 to 2001, which sought to alter a school's thinking about its purpose, its collaboration, and its instruction by establishing and reinforcing a schoolwide Instructional Focus.

In the Brazosport Independent School District, the schools and central office began in 1992 to dramatically improve student achievement and to close the achievement gap for at-risk children. They developed an eight-step process that starts with analyzing disaggregated student performance data and then developing an Instructional Focus to guide changes in teaching and the supports provided to teachers by the school and district.[4]

In 1996, the Kennewick Public Schools in Kennewick, Washington, made literacy the Instructional Focus for all its elementary schools with a goal of having 90 percent of their student reading at or above grade level by the end of the third grade; they met their goal in three years.[5]

The Boston Public Schools was the first major school district to require each school to develop a schoolwide Instructional Focus. Boston has shown significant gains in student performance since instituting this plan for Whole School Change in 1998.

Similar efforts were being undertaken from 1996 to 2000 in New York City's highly recognized Community School District Two. A collaborative project between the Learning Research and Development Center at the University of Pittsburgh, Harvard University, and the district led to dramatic improvement by focusing on instructional improvement through content-driven reform in literacy and mathematics in the district's elementary and middle schools.[5]

Since 1998, Focus on Results has assisted numerous school districts in helping schools establish schoolwide Instructional Focus.

References

1. Kathleen Cotton, "Effective Schooling Practices: A Research Synthesis 1995 Update," NW Regional Educational Laboratory, http://www.nwrel.org/scpd/esp/esp95toc.html.
2. *http://www.ed.gov/pubs/turning/strategy.html#return6*
3. K. Hawley and L. Darling-Hammond, "Rethinking the Use of Teaching Resources: Lessons from High-Performing Schools," Education Evaluation and Policy Analysis (Spring 1998).
4. M. Schmoker, "Brazosport Independent School District: Erasing the Achievement Gap," *The Results Fieldbook: Practical Strategies from Dramatically Improved Schools* (Alexandria VA: Association for Supervision and Curriculum Development, 2001).
5. L. Feilding, N. Kerr, and P. Rosier, *The 90% Reading Goal* (Kennewick, WA: the New Foundation Press, 1998).

Additional research supporting Area 1

"High Performing Learning Communities," CSD 2/LRDC Project, *http://www.lrdc.pitt.edu/hplc/*.

E. Baker, "Multiple Measures: Toward Tiered Systems" (2003).

"CSE Report 607, National Center for Research on Evaluation, Standards, and Student Testing (CRESST)," *http://www.cse.ucla.edu/products/reports_set.htm*.

V. Bernhardt, "Data Analysis for Comprehensive School Improvement (Larchmon, NY: n.p., 1998).

M. Roza, "Eye on Education," Using Data to Improve Schools (Newton, MA: n.p.,1998).

New England Comprehensive Assistance Center and K. Clauset, and J. Frederick, "How to Measure Your School's Effectiveness" in *A Citizen's Notebook for Effective Schools,* Ross Zerchykov, et. al. (Boston, MA: n.p., 1984).

Institute for Responsive Education, http://www.responsiveeducation.org/.

California Center for Effective Schools Web site, *http://effectiveschools.education. ucsb.edu/correlates.html.*

Turning Around Low-Performing Schools: A Guide for State and Local Leaders (May 1998), http://www.ed.gov/pubs/turning/strategy.html#return6.

P. Roy and S. Hord, "Moving NSDC's Staff Development Standards into Practice: Innovation Configurations" (Oxford OH: National Staff Development Council, 2003).

S. C. Chase, "No Excuses: Lessons from Twenty-one High-Performing, High-Poverty Schools" (Washington, D. C.: The Heritage Foundation, 2000), *http://www.noexcuses.org/pdf/noexcuseslessons.pdf.*

J. T. Waters, R. J. Marzano, and B. A. McNulty, *Balanced Leadership: What Thirty Years of Research Tells Us about the Effect of Leadership on Student Achievement.* (Aurora, CO: Mid-continent Research for Education and Learning, 2003). *http://www.mcrel.org/PDF/LeadershipOrganizationDevelopment/5031RR_BalancedLeadership.pdf.*

California Center for Effective Schools Web site, *http://effectiveschools.education. ucsb.edu/correlates.html.*

Turning Around Low-Performing Schools: A Guide for State and Local Leaders (May 1998), http://www.ed.gov/pubs/turning/strategy.html#return6.

American Federation of Teachers Web site, *http://www.aft.org/pubs-reports/downloads/teachers/StandAssessRes.pdf.*

Interstate School Leaders Licensure Consortium, *http://www.umsl.edu/~mpea/Pages/AboutISLLC/AboutISLLC.html#Anchor-63282.*

E-Lead Web site, http://www.e-lead.org/leadership/ld101/standards1.as.

Area 2: Develop Professional Collaboration Teams to Improve Teaching and Learning for All Students.

Professional collaboration teams or professional learning communities under gird many of the current professional development and school improvement efforts.

The NSDC Staff Development Standards calls for "Staff development that improves the learning of all students and organizes adults into learning communities whose goals are aligned with those of the school and district."[1] Building on his experiences as superintendent of the Adlai Stevenson High School District 125 in Lincolnshire Illinois, Richard DuFour[2] calls for the creation of professional learning communities in schools that exhibit the following characteristics:

- Shared mission, vision, and values
- Collective inquiry
- Collaborative teams
- Action orientation and experimentation
- Continuous improvement
- Results orientation

In a 1997 paper, Shirley Hord summarizes the research for effective professional learning communities and noted the importance of collective learning among staff and application of the learning to solutions that address students' needs.[3] She goes on to list the requirements for professional learning communities:

- the collegial and facilitative participation of the principal, who shares leadership—and thus, power and authority—through inviting staff input in decision making
- a shared vision that is developed from staff's unswerving commitment to students' learning and that is consistently articulated and referenced for the staff's work
- collective learning among staff and application of that learning to solutions that address students' needs
- the visitation and review of each teacher's classroom behavior by peers as a feedback and assistance activity to support individual and community improvement
- physical conditions and human capacities that support such an operation

Newmann and Wehlage found in research on more than 1,500 schools in four large-scale studies that interdependent work structures that encourage collaboration enable schools to function as professional communities and enhance student learning.[4]

In analyzing successful restructuring experiments from three elementary schools, Peterson, McCarthey, and Elmore found that changing classroom practice is primarily a problem of continuous learning resulting in improved practice for teachers, not a problem of school organization and where teachers have a shared vision, teaching practice and student learning are successfully connected.[5]

References

1. P. Roy, and S. Hord, "Moving NSDC's Staff Development Standards into Practice: Innovation Configurations" (National Staff Development Council, Oxford OH, 2003) and the NSDC Web site, http://www.nsdc.org/standards/learningcommunities.cfm.
2. R. DuFour and R. Eaker, *Professional Learning Communities at Work: Best Practices for Enhancing Student Achievement,* (Bloomington, IN: National Educational Service and Alexandria, VA: Association of Supervision and Curriculum Development, 1998).
3. S. Hord, *Professional Learning Communities: Communities of Continuous Inquiry and Improvement* (Austin, TX: Southwest Educational Development Laboratory, 18-19, 1998), http://www.sedl.org/pubs/change34/.
4. F. Newmann and G. Wehlage, *Successful School Restructuring: A Report to the Public and Educators* (Madison, WI: Center on Organization and Restructuring of Schools, 1995), 37-48.
5. P. Peterson, S. McCarthey, and R. Elmore, "Learning from School Restructuring," *American Educational Research Journal,* 33 (1996):119-153.

Additional research supporting Area 2

L. M. Earl and L. E. Lee, *Evaluation of the Manitoba School Improvement Program* (1998), http://www.shapethefuture.ca/tempeval.pdf.

P. Roy and S. Hord, "Moving NSDC's Staff Development Standards into Practice: Innovation Configurations" (2003), 13-14.

U.S. Department of Education, *Research, Implementation, and Early Outcomes of the Comprehensive School Reform Demonstration (CSRD) Program* (2003), http://www.ed.gov/rschstat/eval/other/csrd-outcomes/report.pdf.

C. Murphy and D. Lick, Whole-Faculty Study Groups: Creating Professional Learning Communities That Target Student Success (Thousand Oaks, CA: Corwin Press, Third Edition, 2004).

Professional Learning Communities, *www.annenberginstitute.org/images/ProfLearning.pdf* (2004) and C. Coburn (Aug/Sept 2003).

"Rethinking Scale: Moving Beyond Numbers to Deep and Lasting Change," *Educational Researcher* 32 no. 6: 3-12.

C. Coburn, "Rethinking Scale: Moving Beyond Numbers to Deep and Lasting Change."

http://www.aera.net/uploadedFiles/Journals_and_Publications/Journals/Educational_Researcher/3206/3206_Coburn.pdf

A. S. Bryk, J. K. Nagaoka, and F. M. Newmann, *Chicago Classroom Demands for Authentic Intellectual Work: Trends from 1997-1999*, Chicago, Illinois, Consortium on Chicago School Research (Data Brief, October 2000), http://www.consortium-chicago.org/publications/p0f02.html.

Boston Public Schools web site, http://www.boston.k12.ma.us/bps/FOC2.doc.

The Education Trust, Standards in Practice, http://www2.edtrust.org/EdTrust/SIP+Professional+Development/.

Looking at Student Work Web Site, http://www.lasw.org/index.htmlIF.

Annenberg Institute Professional Learning Communities, http://www.annenberginstitute.org/images/ProfLearning.pdf.

Linda Lumsden, "Expectations for Students" http://eric.uoregon.edu/publications/digests/digest116.html.

F. I. Stevens, with J. Grymes, *Opportunity to Learn: Issues of Equity for Poor and Minority Students*, (Washington, DC: National Center for Education Statistics, 1993), *http://www.ncrel.org/sdrs/areas/issues/methods/assment/as8lk18.htm*.

F. Dunne, W. Nave, and A. Lewis, *Critical Friends Groups: Teachers Helping Teachers to Improve Student Learning* no. 28 (December 2000), Research Brief, Phi Delta Kappa Center for Evaluation, Development, and Research, http://www.pdkintl.org/edres/resbul28.htm.

AISR (2004) Professional Learning Communities, www.annenberginstitute.org/images/ProfLearning.pdf.

Area 3: Identify, Learn, and Use Effective Evidence-Based Teaching Practices

In a study[1] published in 1999 on recent scientific research on how people learn, the National Research Council states that learning environments that promote learning, transfer, and competent performance are student centered, knowledge centered, assessment centered, and community centered and that close alignment among these components accelerates learning within and outside school.

- Learner centered—Learners use their current knowledge to construct new knowledge and that what they know and believe at the moment affects how they interpret new information. Learner-centered environments help students make connections between their previous knowledge and their current academic tasks.
- Knowledge centered—In addition to developing general problem solving and thinking skills, learners need well-organized content area knowledge that is presented in ways that are developmentally

appropriate. A knowledge-centered perspective emphasizes depth over breadth to help students develop interconnected pathways within a discipline.

- Assessment centered—Feedback is fundamental to learning and learners need formative assessments that provide opportunities to revise and hence improve the quality of their thinking and learning. If the goal is to enhance understanding, it is not sufficient to provide assessments that focus primarily on memory for facts and formulas.

- Community centered—Learning environments should promote a sense of community where students, teachers, and other interested participants share norms that value learning and high standards that increase opportunities to interact, receive feedback, and learn. Connections between the school and the larger community, including the home, community centers, and after-school clubs, can have important effects on students' academic achievement.

- Finally, there needs to be alignment among the four perspectives of learning environments. They all have the potential to overlap and mutually influence one another. Issues of alignment appear to be very important for accelerating learning both within and outside of schools.

Evidence-based teaching practices that incorporate these principles focus on both how units and lessons are designed and on the strategies and practices teachers use in daily teaching.

Lesson and unit design frameworks such as Understanding by Design[2] and Teaching for Understanding[3] ask teachers to think first about the essential questions, enduring understandings, the standards the unit or lesson is addressing, how students will demonstrate their understanding in authentic performance tasks, and about the learning experiences and formative assessments that will engage students, build understanding and connect with prior knowledge and personal interests, learning styles, and intelligences, and address misconceptions.

Research studies have identified classroom teaching strategies and practices that lead to improvements in student learning. One approach to identifying effective teaching practices is to identify practices that can be used in across subject areas and grade levels. Daniels and Bizar[4] identify six structures for best practice classrooms:

- Integrative units
- Small group activities
- Representing-to-learn (activities to construct meaning and share it)
- Classroom workshop
- Authentic experiences with real world connections
- Reflective assessment

Robert Marzano and others[5] identified nine categories of instructional strategies that improved student performance:

- Identifying similarities and differences
- Summarizing and note taking
- Reinforcing effort and providing recognition
- Homework and practice
- Representing knowledge
- Learning groups
- Setting objectives and providing feedback
- Generating and testing hypotheses
- Cues, questions, and advance organizers

Lauren Resnick and others at the Institute for Learning have developed eight evidence-based principles of learning[6] that support academic rigor, a thinking curriculum, and student understanding and mastery.

- Organize for effort
- Clear expectations
- Recognition of accomplishment
- Fair and credible evaluations

- Academic rigor in a thinking curriculum
- Accountable talk
- Socializing intelligence
- Learning as apprenticeship

The institute has worked with a number of school districts, including NYC District 2, Providence, Denver, and Los Angeles to train teachers, instructional coaches, and administrators to recognize and teach these principles.

Others have identified evidence-based teaching practices that target specific subject areas,[7] grade levels,[8] or groups of students.[9]

Districts, states, and the US Department of Education are emphasizing the importance of using evidence-based teaching practices.

In Boston, whole school instructional improvement is organized around six essentials.[10] Essential number four is "Learn and use evidence-based practices for instruction" and every school must ensure that teachers are using instructional practice effectively and are including ways to integrate what works from other research-based instructional models.

In Kennewick, Washington, a district committed to achieving 95 percent proficiency in reading and math uses an instructional framework[11] that requires teachers to use evidence-based teaching practices and emphasizes the following elements:

- Teacher intentionally plans and instructs for student achievement of essential learnings.
- Each learner is appropriately challenged as the teacher moves students to higher levels of thinking.
- Teacher and student actively participate in the learning and are focused on the lesson.
- The intended learning is achieved.

The Edmonton, Alberta, public schools has identified learning and used effective evidence-based teaching practices as one of four districtwide expectations for supporting teaching and learning.

Many states, such as Maryland,[12] expect schools to design school-improvement plans that incorporate identifying and implementing evidence-based teaching practices.

Federal programs, such as Reading First,[13] now emphasize the importance of using scientifically-based practices and programs to improve student learning.

References

1. J. D. Bransford, A. L. Brown, and R. R. Cocking, eds., *How People Learn: Brain, Mind, Experience, and School* (Washington, D.C.: National Research Council and National Academy Press, 1999), http://books.nap.edu/html/howpeople1/es.html.

2. G. Wiggins, and J. McTighe, Understanding by Design, Association for Supervision and Curriculum Development (Alexandria, VA: n.p., 1998).

3. T. Blythe and Associates The Teaching for Understanding Guide, (San Francisco, CA: Jossey-Bass, Inc., 1998).

4. H. Daniels and M. Bizar, Methods that Matter (Portland ME: Stenhouse Publishers, 1998).

5. R. J. Marzano, D. J. Pickering, and J. Pollock, Classroom Instruction that Works: Research-Based Strategies for Increasing Student Achievement (Alexandria VA: Association for Supervision and Curriculum Development, 2001).

6. L. R. Resnick, "Making America Smarter," *Education Week*, 18 no. 40 (1999): 38-40, http://www.instituteforlearning.org/media/docs/MakingAmericaSmarter.pdf and L. Resnick, M. W. Hall, and fellows of the Institute for Learning, The Principles of Learning: Study Tools for Educators (Pittsburgh, PA: Institute for Learning, Learning Research and Development Center, University of Pittsburgh, 2001). Also available as a CD-ROM.

7. G. Cawelti, ed.,Handbook of Research on Improving Student Achievement, Third Edition (Arlington, VA: Educational Research Service, 2004).

8. For example, see L. M. Wilson and H. W. Hadley Wilson Horch, *Implications of Brain Research for Teaching Young Adolescents,* National Middle School Association (September 2002), http://www.nmsa.org/research/articles/res_articles_sept002.htm.

9. For examples, see H. C. Waxman and K. Tellez, *Effective Teaching Practices for English Language Learners* (2002). LSS Spotlight on Success, no. 705. Philadelphia, PA. Laboratory for Student Success http://www.temple.edu/LSS/pdf/spotlights/700/spot705.pdf. and Kerka, S. (2003). *Alternatives for At-Risk and Out-of-School Youth.* ERIC Digest no. 248. http://www.cete.org/acve/docgen.asp?tbl=digests&ID=134.

10. http://www.boston.k12.ma.us/bps/FOC2.doc.

11. L. Fielding, N. Kerr, and P. Rosier, *Delivering on the Promise of 95% Reading and Math Goals,* (Kennewick, WA: the New Foundation Press, Inc., 2004).

12. http://mdk12.org/process/10steps/6/index.html. http://www.ed.gov/programs/readingfirst/index.html.

13. http://www.ed.gov/programs/readingfirst/index.html.

Additional research supporting Area 3

See best practices from School Improvement in Maryland, http://mdk12.org/instruction/index.html, Arizona, http://azk12.nau.edu/bestpractices/, and Georgia, http://www.glc.k12.ga.us/trc/cluster.asp?mode=browse&intPathID=3349.

A. C. Picucci, A. Brownson, R. Kahlett, and A. Sobeel, *Driven to Succeed: High-Performing, High-Poverty, Turnaround Middle Schools, Volume 1, Cross-Case Analysis* (Austin, TX: the Charles A. Dana Center, University of Texas at Austin, 2004).

D. J. Briars, D. J. and L. B. Resnick, L. B., *Standards, Assessment—and*

What Else? The Essential Elements of Standards-Based School Improvement, CSE Technical Report 528, Los Angeles: Center for the Study of Evaluation, UCLA.

B. Briars and L. Resnick, "Standards, Assessments, and What Else? Essential Elements of Standards-Based School Improvement," http://www.cse.ucla.edu/CRESST/Reports/TECH528.pdf See, for example, Maryland's guidelines for choosing strategies, *http://mdk12.org/process/10steps/6/index.html.*

See Edmonton's expectations, http://superbresults.epsb.ca/cf/memoattach/Expectations_04_05.pdf.

J. T. Fouts, C. Brown, and Thieman, Classroom Instruction in Gates Grantee Schools: A Baseline Report (Fouts & Associates, L.L.C. for the Bill and Melinda Gates Foundation, 2002), http://www.gatesfoundation.org/nr/ downloads/ed/researchevaluation/ClassroomInstruction.pdf.

L. Martin, M. L. Abbott, T. Jeffrey, and J. T. Fouts, *Constructivist Teaching and Student Achievement: The Results of a School-Level Classroom Observation Study in Washington* (Technical Report #5, Washington School Research Center, 2003). http://www.spu.edu/wsrc/ObservationStudy-2-13-03.pdf.

L. Fielding, N. Kerr, and P. Rosier, *Delivering on the Promise of 95% Reading and Math Goals* (Kennewick, WA: the New Foundation Press, Inc., 2004).

The work in Community District Two is described in the article by Richard Elmore, "Building A New Structure for School Leadership," *American Educator* Vol. 24 (Winter 1999-2000): 6-19.

T. Guskey, Results-Oriented Professional Development: In search of an Optimal Mix of Effective Practices (1995), http://www.ncrel.org/sdrs/ areas/rpl_esys/pdlitrev.htm.

D. Sparks and G. Cawelti, ed., "Focusing Staff Development on Improving the Learning for All Students," *Handbook of Research on Improving Student achievement*, Third Edition (Arlington, VA: Educational Research Service, 2004). http://www.nsdc.org/standards/about/index.cfm.

L. Darling-Hammond, "Teacher Quality and Student Achievement," *Education Policy Analysis Archives*. 8 no. 1, (2000), http://epaa.asu.edu/epaa/v8n1/.

Georgia Standards for School Performance, http://www.doe.k12.ga.us/support/improvement/gspr.asp.

Area 4: Create a Targeted Professional Development Plan that Builds Expertise in Selected Evidence-Based Practices

Creating and implementing a targeted professional development plan for selected evidence-based practices assumes that a school has already analyzed its student performance data to identify strengths and challenges against specific improvement goals, defined a schoolwide Instructional Focus, and selected a small set of evidence-based strategies to master and use throughout the school.

"Targeted" and "selected" are the important terms. Most school improvement plans and their associated professional development plans are neither targeted nor focused on selected strategies. Instead, Mike Schmoker[1] faults the typical planning process which leads to "plans that are oversized, imprecise, and an obstacle to improvement—setting off a riot of activities, which supplant the work of teachers to create, adapt, use and evaluate lessons and strategies aimed at helping higher proportions of students master essential standards."

States and districts are changing the planning process to increase student learning. The state of Washington[2] now requires that each school's School

Improvement Plan and process include Focused Professional Development aligned with the school's common focus, objectives, and high expectations and based on high-need areas. The Georgia Standards for School Performance[3] call for schools to have "prioritized content for professional learning focused on teacher and student needs that address the elements of equity, quality teaching, and family involvement."

Implementing a targeted professional development plan that builds expertise in selected evidence-based practices is one of eight district expectations for schools for 2004-2005 in the Edmonton, Alberta, Public Schools.[4]

References

1. M. Schmoker, "The Real Causes of Higher Achievement" *SEDL Letter 14:2* (2002), http://www.sedl.org/pubs/sedletter/v14n02/welcome.html.

2. *Research Based Effective Practices in Professional Development,* Washington State Guide, found in www.k12.wa.us/Conferences/JanConf2005/CallforPresenters.doc.

3. Georgia Standards for School Performance, http://www.doe.k12.ga.us/support/improvement/gspr.asp.

4. See Edmonton's expectations, http://superbresults.epsb.ca/cf/memoattach/Expectations_04_05.pdf.

Additional research supporting Area 4

L. Fielding, N. Kerr, and P. Rosier, *The 90% Reading Goal* (Kennewick, WA: the New Foundation Press, Inc., 1998).

Boston Public Schools, http://boston.k12.ma.us/teach/offices.pdf.

D. Sparks, "Focusing Staff Development on Improving the Learning for All Students" *Handbook of Research on Improving Student Achievement,* Third Edition, G. Cawelti, ed. (Arlington, VA: Educational Research Service, 2004).

M. B. Haslam and C. P. Seremet, Strategies for Improving Professional Development: A Guide for School District (Arlington, VA: New American Schools, 2001), http://www.naschools.org/uploadedfiles/Strategies%20for%20I mproving%20Professional%20Development.pdf.

Education Development Center, The Teaching Firm: Where Productive Work and Learning Converge, (Newton, MA: Education Development Center, Inc., 1998).

Washington State Professional Development Planning Guide, Part I—Teacher Professional Development. Effective, Research-Based Practices in Professional Development at http://www.k12.wa.us/ProfDev/default.aspx.

M. B. Haslam and C. P. Seremet, Strategies for Improving Professional Development: A Guide for School District (Arlington, VA: New American Schools, 2001), http://www.naschools.org/uploadedfiles/Strategies%20for%20I mproving%20Professional%20Development.pdf.

P. Roy and S. Hord, Moving NSDC's Staff Development Standards into Practice: Innovation Configurations (Oxford OH: National Staff Development Council, 2003) and the NSDC web site http://www.nsdc.org/standards/learningcommunities.cfm.

School Communities that Work, "Generally Accepted Principles of Teaching and Learning and their Implications for Local Education Support Systems" (2002), http://www.schoolcommunities.org/portfolio/gaptl.html#principles.

Edmonton Public Schools Expectations, http://superbresults.epsb.ca/cf/memoattach/central_expectations_04_05.pdf.

Edmonton Public Schools Consulting Services, http://consultingservices.epsb.net/classroom.cfm.

National Center for Education Statistics, America's Teachers: Profile of a Profession, 1993-94 (NCES 97-460), Washington, DC: U.S. Department of Education, Office of Educational Research and Improvement (July 1997).

National Staff Development Council, http://www.nsdc.org/standards/strategies.cfm.

L. Fielding, N. Kerr, and P. Rosier, *Delivering on the Promise of 95% Reading and Math Goals*, (Kennewick, WA: the New Foundation Press, Inc., 2004).

Institute for Learning, http://www.instituteforlearning.org/howwk.html.

Principals Partnership, http://www.principalspartnership.com/feature203.html.

B. A. VonVillas, "Improving the Way We Observe Classrooms," The School Administrator Web Edition (2004), http://www.aasa.org/publications/sa/2004_09/focus_vonvillas.htm.

L. Darling-Hammond, "Teacher Quality and Student Achievement," Education Policy Analysis Archives, 8 no. 1 (2000), http://epaa.asu.edu/epaa/v8n1/.

Indiana Department of Education, http://www.doe.state.in.us/asap/prodev2.html#anchor155967.

T. B. Guskey, "Does It Make a Difference? Evaluating Professional Development," Educational Leadership, 59 no. 6 (2002): 45-51 and found online at http://www.nsrfharmony.org/guskey.pdf.

C. Murphy and D. Lick, Whole-Faculty Study Groups: Creating Professional Learning Communities that Target Student Success (Thousand Oaks, CA: Corwin Press, Third Edition, 2004).

L. Fielding, N. Kerr, and P. Rosier, *Delivering on the Promise of 95% Reading and Math Goals* (Kennewick, WA: the New Foundation Press, Inc., 2004).

L. Darling-Hammond, "Teacher Quality and Student Achievement," Education Policy Analysis Archives, 8 no. 1 (2000), http://epaa.asu.edu/epaa/v8n1/.

P. D. Tucker and J. H. Stronge, "Measure for Measure: Using Student Test Results in Teacher Evaluations" American School Board Journal, 188 no. 9 (September 2001): 34-37.

North Carolina Standards for Teacher Evaluation, http://www.ncpublicschools.org/evalpsemployees/teacherstand.htm.

Area 5: Re-align Resources to Support the Instructional Focus

Much research over the past decade has supported aligning resources to support high student achievement. For example, the 1995 Research Synthesis on Effective Schooling Practices by Kathleen Cotton at the Northwest Regional Educational Laboratory[1] states that effective schools

- Group students in ways that promote effective instruction
- Assure that school time is use for learning
- Continually strive to improve instructional effectiveness

Provide programs and support to help high-needs students achieve school success and effective districts

- Establish policies and procedures that support excellence and equity in student performance
- Encourage, support, and monitor school improvement efforts

A 2002 study of high-performing, high-poverty, turn-around middle schools found[2] that schools driven to succeed are committed to supporting high quality teaching and learning by

- Implementing thoughtful organizational structures such as student teaming, block schedules, and teacher common planning time and building capacity
- Providing extra services and supports to individual students

In reviewing two decades of research, the School Communities that Work Task Force at the Annenberg Institute for School Reform concluded[3] that three district level functions are essential for school success:

- Provide schools, students, and teachers with needed support and timely interventions
- Ensure that schools have the power and resources to make good decisions
- Make decisions and hold people throughout the system accountable by using indicators of school and district performance and practices

In a 1993 research study of the ways in which districts supported school reform in San Francisco Bay Area, McLaughlin and Talbert found[4] that support for school reform throughout the district by aligning structures and resources to provide a coherent focus on teaching and learning and support for professional learning, instructional improvements, and data-based inquiry and accountability.

The US Department of Education's monograph, Turning Around Low-Performing Schools: A Guide for State and Local Leaders (May 1998),[5] concludes "turning around schools requires tough choices about resource allocation. Creating a true focus on learning in a school may cost jobs and require major shifts in financial resources. Districts and schools must pay attention to how they allocate staff, budgets, materials, and space. Turning around a low-performing school may require that resources long spent on aides, paraprofessionals, and other specialists be moved to support a school's Instructional Focus."

Gordon Cawelti, in a summary of his research[6] on six high-performing school systems, says a key characteristic of these districts was restructuring the organization linking people to results. This restructuring includes shifting authority, responsibility, and resources for change down to the school level and redefining central office roles from control and compliance to support.

In Boston,[7] one of the six essentials driving the district push to improve performance for all students is that schools must align all resources with their Instructional Focus—focusing on three critical areas—staff, schedule, and budget. Each of these should be developed and aligned to enable the school to carry out focused instruction and professional development.

References

1. Kathleen Cotton, Effective Schooling Practices: A Research Synthesis 1995 Update (NW Regional Educational Laboratory, 1995), http://www.nwrel.org/scpd/esp/esp95toc.html.

2. A. C. Picucci, A. Brownson, R. Kahlett, and A. Sobeel, Driven to Succeed: High-Performing, High-Poverty, Turnaround Middle Schools, Volume 1, Cross-Case Analysis (Austin, TX: the Charles A. Dana Center, University of Texas at Austin, 2002).

3. Annenberg Institute for School Reform, School Communities that Work for Results and Equity (2002), http://www.schoolcommunities.org/portfolio/results_equity.html.

4. M. McLaughlin and J. Talbert, "Reforming Districts: How Districts Support School Reform, A Research Report," Center for the Study of Teaching and Policy, University of Washington (2003), http://depts.washington.edu/ctpmail/PDFs/ReformingDistricts-09-2003.pdf.

5. Turning Around Low-Performing Schools: A Guide for State and Local Leaders (May 1998), http://www.ed.gov/pubs/turning/strategy.html #return6.

6. G. Cawelti, ed., "A Synthesis of Research on High-Performing School Systems," Handbook of Research on Improving Student Achievement, Third Edition (Arlington, VA: Educational Research Service, 2004).

7. Boston Public Schools, http://www.boston.k12.ma.us/bps/ FOC2.doc.

Additional research supporting Area 5

K. H. Miles and L. Darling-Hammond, "Rethinking the Allocation of Teaching Resources: Some Lessons from High-Performing Schools," *Educational Evaluation and Policy Analysis*, 20 no. 1 (Spring 1998): 9-29, *www.cpre.org/Publications/rr38.pdf.*

A. Odden and S. Archibald, *Reallocating Resources: How to Boost Student Achievement Without Asking for More* (Thousand Oaks, CA: Corwin Press, 2001).

P. Roy and S. Hord, Moving NSDC's Staff Development Standards into Practice: Innovation Configurations, (Oxford, OH: National Staff Development Council, 2003) and the NSDC web site, http://www.nsdc.org/standards/learning communities.cfm.

M. Roza and P. T. Hill, "How Within-District Spending Inequities Help Some Schools Fail," in *Brookings Papers on Education Policy: 2004,* ed. Diane Ravitch (Washington DC: Brookings Institution Press, 2004), www.brookings.edu/press/books/abstracts/BPEP/200405.pdf

"School Communities that Work," *First Steps to a Level Playing Field: An Introduction to Student-Based Budgeting* (2002), Annenberg Institute for School Reform, http://www.schoolcommunities.org/portfolio/sbb.html

K. H. Miles, Rethinking the Use of Teaching Resources, *School Business Affairs*, 63 no. 6 (1997): 35-40.

A. Odden and S. Archibald, op. cit., *Reallocating Resources: How to Boost Student Achievement Without Asking for More* (Thousand Oaks, CA: Corwin Press, 2001).

Center for Collaborative Education, *"How Boston Pilot Schools Use Freedom Over Budget, Staffing, and Scheduling to Meet Student Needs"* (2001), www.ccebos.org/pilot_resource_study_011015.pdf.

L. Fielding, N. Kerr, and P. Rosier, *Delivering on the Promise of 95% Reading and Math Goals,* (Kennewick, WA: the New Foundation Press, Inc., 2004).

A. Odden and S. Archibald, *Reallocating Resources: How to Boost Student Achievement Without Asking for More* (Thousand Oaks, CA: Corwin Press, 2001).

Listed in K. H. Miles's *Rethinking School Resources,* New American Schools, http://www.naschools.org/uploadedfiles/rethinking-resources.pdf.

K. H. Miles, *Rethinking School Resources,* New American Schools, http://www.naschools.org/uploadedfiles/rethinking-resources.pdf.

K. H. Miles, *Matching Spending with Strategy: Aligning District Spending to Support a Strategy of Comprehensive School Reform,* New American Schools, http://www.naschools.org/uploadedfiles/Matching.pdf.

Area 6: Engage Families and the Community in Supporting the Instructional Focus

Swap[1] has described four different models for parent involvement: protective, school-to-home transmission, curriculum enrichment, and partnership model.

- Protective model—protects the school from parental interference— *Least effective*
- School-to-home transmission model—enlist parents in supporting the school's mission
- Curriculum enrichment model—draw on parents' knowledge and experiences to inform instruction

- Partnership model—work together to accomplish a common mission—for all children in school to achieve success—*Most effective*

Development and implementation of a partnership model for home-school relationships requires, according to Swap, the presence of four essential elements.

- Two-way communication processes established.
- The recognition that learning is enhanced at home and at school.
- Mutual support across home and school.
- Parents and educators make joint decisions at various levels.

Joyce Epstein, director of the Center on School, Family, and Community Partnerships at Johns Hopkins University, has identified six major types[2] of family and community involvement with schools:

- *Parenting.* Assist families with parenting skills, family support, understanding child, and adolescent development, and setting home conditions to support learning at each age and grade level. Assist schools in understanding families' backgrounds, cultures, and goals for children.
- *Communicating.* Communicate with families about school programs and student progress. Create two-way communication channels between school and home.
- *Volunteering.* Improve recruitment, training, activities, and schedules to involve families as volunteers and as audiences at the school or in other locations. Enable educators to work with volunteers who support students and the school.
- *Learning at Home.* Involve families with their children in academic learning at home, including homework, goal setting, and other curriculum-related activities. Encourage teachers to design homework that enables students to share and discuss interesting tasks.

- *Decision Making.* Include families as participants in school decisions, governance, and advocacy activities through school councils or improvement teams, committees, and parent organizations.
- *Collaborating with the Community.* Coordinate resources and services for families, students, and the school with community groups, including businesses, agencies, cultural and civic organizations, and colleges or universities. Enable all to contribute service to the community.

Epstein describes some of the ways family and community involvement is supporting the Instructional Focus in schools in the National Network of Partnership Schools:

Reading

- Offer workshop sessions on reading
- Organize reading volunteers
- Help parents strengthen students' reading skills and encourage reading for pleasure at home
- Conduct reading-partner programs regularly with a variety of volunteers
- Hold special reading events
- Provide books to students and families to improve the early literacy skills of preschool and kindergarten children.

Writing

- Offer workshops in the writing process
- Organize activities that engage parents in writing
- Arrange presentations by local authors and
- Hold celebrations of student writing before family and community audiences
- Involve parents in creating books and videos about their lives and experiences writing poems about their children, and then presenting their work to their children.

Math

- Organize math night events for parents and students, community connections
- Hold information sessions for parents on math curriculum and assessments
- Provide homework support conduct teacher-led math sessions on ways to help students with math at home
- Distribute take-home bags of math materials and information on state standards
- Use community connections for real applications, such as following a local moving man to estimate the weight and cost of a moving job
- Organize after-school workshops for parents and students to practice together for the state math test

In a synthesis of research on improving student achievement, Walberg and Fink[3] cite parental involvement as an effective general practice for enhancing learning when schools encourage parents to stimulate their children's intellectual development by engaging in activities such as encouraging and discussing reading.

A 1995 Research Synthesis on Effective Schooling Practices[4] states that a key characteristic of effective schools is parental involvement where administrators and teachers

- Communicate repeatedly to parents that their involvement can greatly enhance their children's school performance, regardless of their own level of education
- Offer parents different options for their involvement
- Strongly encourage parents to become involved in activities that support the instructional program
- Provide parents with information and techniques for helping students learn

- Establish and maintain regular, frequent home-school communications that provides parents with information about student progress and calls attention to any areas of difficulty
- Involve community members in classroom activities
- Make special efforts to involve the parents of disadvantaged, racial minority, and language minority students, who are often underrepresented among parents involved in the schools

In Kennewick, Washington, the district[5] has extended its focus on reading to the aged zero-to-four children to strengthen reading skills of entering kindergarten students. They partner with the Reading Foundation to support family literacy activities.

In a study, "Parents and Schooling in the 1990s," Flaxman and Inger[6] found five primary principles that apply to parent involvement in schools:

1. Involving parents in their children's education improves student achievement and behavior, but parent involvement is most effective when it is comprehensive, well planned, and long lasting.
2. Parent involvement develops over time as an integral part of a school improvement or restructuring strategy, rather than a remedial intervention.
3. The benefits of parent involvement are not confined to early childhood or the elementary grades. There are strong, positive effects from involving parents continuously through high school.
4. Parents do not have to be well-educated themselves in order to help.
5. Children from low-income and minority families benefit greatly when schools involve parents.

References

1. S. M. Swap, Developing Home-School Partnerships: From Concepts to Practice. (New York: Teacher College Press,

1993), found in Leadership Module for Family-School Partnerships: Creating Essential Connections for Children's Reading and Learning by Sandy Christenson, University of Minnesota, http://www.gse.harvard.edu/hfrp/content/projects/fine/resources/materials/leadership_module.doc.

2. J. L. Epstein and K. C. Salinas, "Partnering with Families and Communities" Educational Leadership, 61 no. 8 (2004): 12-18.

3. H. J. Walberg and S. J. Paik, "Effective General Practices," *Handbook of Research on Improving Student Achievement*, Third Edition, ed. G. Cawelti (Arlington, VA: Educational Research Service, 2004).

4. Kathleen Cotton, Effective Schooling Practices: A Research Synthesis 1995 Update, NW Regional Educational Laboratory (1995), http://www.nwrel.org/scpd/esp/esp95toc.html.

5. L. Fielding, N. Kerr, and P. Rosier, Delivering on the Promise of 95% Reading and Math Goals (Kennewick, WA: the New Foundation Press, Inc., 2004).

6. E. Flaxman and M. Inger, Parents and Schooling in the 1990s, The ERIC Review, 1 no. 3 (September 1991): 2-6.

Additional research supporting Area 6

J. L. Epstein, School, Family, and Community Partnerships: Preparing Educators and Improving Schools (Boulder CO: Westview Press, 2001).

National Standards for Parent/Family Involvement Programs, http://www.pta.org/parentinvolvement/standards/pdf/stndeng.pdf.

O. C. Moles, Building School-Family Partnerships for Learning: Workshops for Urban Educators (Washington, DC: Office of Educational Research and Improvement [OERI], U.S. Department of Education, 1993). Citation found in Leadership Module for Family-School Partnerships: Creating Essential Connections for Children's Reading and Learning by Sandy Christenson, University of Minnesota, http://

www.gse.harvard.edu/hfrp/content/projects/fine/resources/materials/leadership_module.doc.

National Network of Partnership Schools. Type 2 Research Brief. "Partnership Activities Help Improve Schools' Math Proficiency Test Scores," adapted from S. B. Sheldon and J. L. Epstein (2001). Focus on Math Achievement: Effects of Family and Community Involvement. An earlier version of this paper was presented at the 2001 annual meeting of the American Sociological Association, Anaheim, CA, http://www.csos.jhu.edu/p2000/partnership_awards/2003/Research/type2_research_briefs/ttype2k4a.htm.

National Network of Partnership Schools. Type 2 Research Brief. "Home, School, and Community Effects on the Academic Achievement of African-American Adolescents," adapted from Mavis G. Sanders and Jerald R. Herting (2000). "Gender and the Effects of School, Family, and Church Support on the Academic Achievement of African-American Urban Youth" in Schooling Students Placed at Risk: Research, Policy, and Practice in the Education of Poor and Minority Adolescents, ed. Mavis G. Sanders, New Jersey: Lawrence-Erlbaum Publishers.

A. Erickson, Looking at Student Work Together: A Preliminary Report of the Annenberg Institute Working Group on Teacher and Parent Collaboration in Looking at Student Work (1999), http://www.annenberginstitute.org/publications/ACPBCaseStudies/toc.html.

Parents focused on improving student achievement (2003), http://compass.epsb.net/09_06_2003/focused.html.

Education Trust, http://www2.edtrust.org/EdTrust/SIP+Professional+Development/

A Compact for Learning: An Action Handbook for Family-School-Community Partnerships, *http://www.ed.gov/pubs/Compact/*.

Area 7: Create an Internal Accountability System

Ken Jones, in a 2004 article in Phi Delta Kappan[1], argues that schools must develop an internal accountability system to be an effective collective enterprise. Schools must take responsibility for developing goals and priorities based on the ongoing collection and analysis of data; monitor performance, and report its findings and actions to its public. He proposes that the internal accountability system focus on four areas—student learning; opportunity to learn; responsiveness to students, parents, community; and organizational capacity.

In the area of student learning, he recommends a system that

- is primarily intended to improve student learning
- aligns with local curricula
- emphasizes applied learning and thinking skills, not just declarative knowledge and basic skills
- embodies the principle of multiple measures, including a variety of formats

In a 2002 paper,[2] Richard Elmore draws on research on high-performing schools to state that "internal accountability precedes external accountability and is a precondition for any process of improvement." Internal accountability is more than analyzing data. "Schools do not succeed in responding to external cues or pressures unless they have their own internal system for reaching agreement on good practice and for making that agreement evident in organization and pedagogy." Schools with strong internal accountability systems have a high degree of alignment among individual teachers about what they can do and about their responsibility for the improvement of student learnings, shared expectations among teachers, administrators, and students about what constitutes good work and a set of processes for observing whether these expectations are being met.

Most schools are different from this. A 1999 research study[3] by the Consortium for Policy Research in Education found that the attitudes, values, and beliefs of individual teachers and administrators about what their students are capable of learning are more influential in determining a school's accountability system than are external policies. The study indicates that an external accountability system must be supported by changed perceptions of individual responsibility and collective expectations within schools for improvement.

According to WestEd researchers,[4] the advantages of a locally tailored accountability system over a state accountability system are that a local system can yield a more complete and nuanced picture of schools, provide information detailed enough to guide district decisions, and inform decisions about curriculum and instruction.

Susan Fuhrman reports in a 2001 book[5] that schools with a strong internal accountability system already in place were more successful implementing state-mandated accountability systems.

In Edmonton, Alberta, each school[6] is expected to have an internal accountability system that uses external and local data as a lens for decision making.

Along with the other elementary schools in the district, the Washington Elementary School in Kennewick, Washington,[7] with 50 percent of its students in poverty, built an internal accountability system where at least one adult is responsible for every child's growth and specific interventions if they are needed. In the spring 2001, the school set a new district record with 96 percent of all students meeting or exceeding the standard.

In Clarke County, Nevada, the district and schools have created an internal accountability system[8] to establish a results-oriented educational system in which all educators and students (with parent and family support) are held accountable for student learning. The units of analysis and accountability are the district, the region, the school/principal, the grade level/department, the teacher, and the student. Schools and students are to be held accountable for meeting the annual goals and targets. Data-driven accountability decisions are made based on

- To what extent are students/schools meeting specified achievement targets?
- Which students/teachers/grade levels/schools/curricular areas need to improve?
- To what extent have achievement gaps been reduced?
- To what extent are Access, School Improvement, and School-Home Relations goals being met?

References

1. K. Jones, "A Balanced School Accountability Model: An Alternative to High-Stakes Testing," *Phi Delta Kappan,* 85 no. 8 (2004): 584-590, http://www.pdkintl.org/kappan/k0404jon.htm
2. R. E. Elmore, "Standards and Achievement: The Imperative for Professional Development in Education" (Albert Shanker Institute, 2002), www.shankerinstitute.org/Downloads/Bridging_Gap.pdf.
3. C. Abelmann and R. Elmore, with J. Even, K. Kenyon, and J. Marshall, When Accountability Knocks, Will Anyone Answer? Research Report No.42, Consortium for Policy Research in Education, March 1999, No. RR-042, http://www.cpre.org/Publications/rr42.pdf
4. E. W. Crane, S. N. Rabinowitz, and J. Zimmerman, *Locally Tailored Accountability: Building on Your State System in the Era of NCLB,* Knowledge Brief, WestEd (2004), http://www.wested.org/online_pubs/KN-04-01.pdf.
5. S. H. Fuhrman, *From the Capitol to the Classroom: Standards-Based Reform in the States* (Chicago, IL: University of Chicago Press, National Society for the Study of Education, 2001).

6. See Edmonton's expectations, http://superbresults.epsb.ca/cf/ memoattach/Expectations_04_05.pdf.
7. P. W. Rosier, "Our Goal: 90 Percent Reading," *The School Administrator Web Edition*, January 2002, http://www.aasa.org/publications/sa/2002_01/rosier.htm.
8. Clarke County, Nevada, http://ccsd.net/schools/perkins/student%20 handbook.htm.

Additional research supporting Area 7

Every Child Reading: An Action Plan of the Learning First Alliance, June 1998, http://www.readbygrade3.com/readbygrade3co/lfa.htm.

Guidance for the Reading First Program.
http://www.ed.gov/programs/readingfirst/guidance.pdf.

Illinois Reading First Application. www.isbe.state.il.us/nclb/pdfs/ilreading.pdf.

M. Schmoker, *The Results Fieldbook* (Alexandria, VA: Association for Supervision and Curriculum Development, 2001).

R. Marzano, What Works in Schools: Translating Research into Action (Alexandria, VA: Association for Supervision and Curriculum Development, 2003).

D. B. Reeves, "Accountability-Based Reforms Should Lead to Better Teaching and Learning Period," *Harvard Education Letter* (March/April 2002).

R. J. Marzano, D. J. Pickering, and J. Pollock, *Classroom Instruction that Works: Research-Based Strategies for Increasing Student Achievement* (Alexandria, VA: Association for Supervision and Curriculum Development, 2001).

National Board for Professional Teaching Standards, Middle Childhood Generalist Standards (2001), http://www.nbpts.org/pdf/mc_gen_2ed.pdf.

L. Fielding, N. Kerr, and P. Rosier, *Delivering on the Promise of 95% Reading and Math Goals* (Kennewick, WA: the New Foundation Press, Inc., 2004).

R. F. Elmore, with the assistance of Deanna Burney, Investing in Teacher Learning: Staff Development and Instructional Improvement in Community School District #2 (New York City, 1997), http://www.iadb.org/int/DRP/ing/Red4/Documents/ElmoreAbril4-5-2002ing.pdf.

M. Schmoker, *The Results Fieldbook* (Alexandria, VA: Association for Supervision and Curriculum Development, 2001).

J. P. Kotter and D. S. Cohen, *The Heart of Change* (Boston, MA: Harvard Business School Press, 2002).

J. A. Conger and R. N. Kanungo, *Charismatic Leadership: The Elusive Factor in Organizational Effectiveness* (San Francisco: Jossey-Bass, 1988), http://www.coastwiseconsulting.com/Charismatic%20Leadership%20-%20OCRed.pdf.

M. M. Schmoker, *Results: The Key to Continuous School Improvement* (Alexandria, VA: Association for Supervision and Curriculum Development, 1996).

D. Sparks, "The Singular Power of One Goal," *Journal of Staff Development*, 20 no. 1 (Winter 1999): 54-58.

R. S. Rubin, "Will the Real SMART Goals Please Stand Up?" *The Industrial-Organizational Psychologist*, 39 no. 4 (2002), http://siop.org/tip/backissues/TIPApr02/03rubin.htm

A. Conzemius and J. O'Neill, *The Handbook for SMART School Teams* (Bloomington, IN: National Educational Service, 2002).

See Edmonton's SMARTe targets and expectations, http://superbresults.epsb.ca/cf/StudentAchievementTargets.cfm

L. Fielding, N. Kerr, and P. Rosier, *Delivering on the Promise of 95% Reading and Math Goals,* Kennewick, WA: the New Foundation Press, Inc., 2004).

Appendix C

Bibliography

Chapter 1

Boston Plan for Excellence: www.bpe.org.

Boston Public Schools: boston.k12.ma.us.

National Middle Grades Forum: http://www.mgforum.org/Improvingschools/STW/STWbackground.htm.

Blue Ribbon Schools: http://www.ed.gov/programs/nclbbrs/contacts.html.

Carter, Samuel. *No Excuses: Lessons from Twenty-one High-Performing, High-Poverty Schools.* Washington: Heritage Foundation, 2000.

Reeves, Doug. *Accountability in Action.* Englewood: Advanced Learning Press, 2000.

Howard, Jeff. Getting Smart: The Social Construct of Intelligence. Lexington: the Efficacy Institute, 1992.

Elmore, R. Building a New Structure for School Leadership. *American Educator,* American Federation of Teachers, Winter 1999-2000.

Chapter 2

Murphy, Carlene. Finding Time for Faculty Study Groups. *Journal of Staff Development* 3, 1997.

Annenberg Institute: www.studio.aisr.brown.edu

Chapter 3

Resnick, L., M. W. Hall, and fellows of the Institute for Learning. The Principles of Learning: Study Tools for Educators. 2001. Also available as a CD-ROM. Pittsburgh, PA: Institute for Learning, Learning Research and Development Center, University of Pittsburgh.

International Network of Principals' Centers: http://www.gse.harvard.edu/principals/network.htm.

Open Space Technology: http://www.openspaceworld.org.

Association for Supervision and Curriculum Development: www.ascd.org.

Chapter 4

National Writing Project: http://www.writingproject.org/.

Barth, Roland. The Culture Builder. *Educational Leadership, Volume 59, No. 8,* 2002.

Chapter 5

Miles, K. and L. Darling-Hammond. "Rethinking the Use of Teaching Resources: Lessons from High Performing Schools." *Education Evaluation and Policy Analysis.* Spring 1998.

Chapter 6

Epstein, Joyce et al. *School, Family, and Community Partnerships. Caring for the Children We Share.* Thousand Oaks: Corwin Press. Inc., 1997.

Chapter 7

Schmoker, Michael. *Results: The Key to Continuous School Improvement,* Alexandria: ASCD, 1996.

Schlechty, P. *Inventing Better Schools: An Action Plan for Educational Reform.* San Francisco: Jossey Bass, 2001.

Chapter 8

Cudeiro, Amalia. "Superintendents and Student Achievement: Lessons Learned from Real Success Stories. "Focus on Results, 2002.

Chapter 9

Stigler, James and J. Hiebert. The Teaching Gap: Best Ideas from the World's Teachers for Improving Education in the Classroom. New York: The Free Press, 1999.

Education Trust: http://www2.edtrust.org/edtrust.

Elmore, R. School Reform from the Inside Out: Policy, Practice, and Performance. Cambridge: Harvard Educational Publishers Group, 2004.

2712
gift